Money for Nothing

And Your Stocks for **FREE!**

The Financial Catch-Up Strategy from

Canada's Youngest Retiree

Derek Foster

FOSTER, UNDERHILL FINANCIAL PRESS

Library and Archives Canada Cataloguing in Publication

Foster, Derek, 1970–
    Money for nothing : and your stocks for free / Derek Foster.

ISBN 978-0-9736960-2-8

    1. Retirement income—Planning.   2. Investments.
    3. Finance, Personal.

I. Title.
HG179.F665 2008   332.024'014   C2008-904896-2ISBN

Published by
Foster, Underhill Financial Press
900 Greenbank Road, Suite 508
Ottawa, ON K2J 4P6
Canada
Phone toll free at: 1 888 686 STOP (1 888 686 7867)
or 613 823 2143
www.stopworking.ca

Design/formatting/production: WeMakeBooks.ca
Printed and bound in Canada

National Praise for Derek Foster

LEGAL DISCLAIMER

This book is intended to show you a strategy that you might want to consider for investing.

However, you must realize that I am not a professional with regard to any of the information I've provided in this book. I am merely presenting a strategy that I feel might be of interest to you. I am not an expert in economic, legal, taxation, investing, realty, or any other financial or related matters. The examples I provide are just that—examples. These are intended for illustrative purposes only. They are not an indication of what rate of return or future amount of money you might have if you followed the specific examples. They are only presented to illustrate the general concepts. Before initiating any of the strategies outlined, seek the advice of a competent professional to help you.

The book is intended as a general guide and should not be viewed as the ultimate source for financial information. Further research is needed and assistance must be sought from a qualified expert, before any action is taken by the reader. For further information, there is a recommended reading list at the back of this book. The information in these books might be incomplete, inaccurate, or out of date, so the reader should verify any of this information before acting on it.

For full disclosure, I must say that I (Derek Foster) own many of the securities mentioned in this book. The reader must also understand that any investing activity entails certain degrees of risk. Although lists of securities are presented in the book, the reader must understand that these securities do carry risk and should seek the advice from a qualified expert before acting upon any of the information.

Furthermore, this book might contain various errors, omissions, or mistakes of either a typographical nature or within the content itself. The reader must not rely on the accuracy of any of the information given, but should seek proper verification.

The author (Derek Foster) and the publisher (Foster Underhill Financial Press) shall have neither liability nor responsibility to any person or other legal entity with respect to any sort of loss or damage or perceived damage caused, or alleged to have been caused by the information provided in this book. By reading this, you fully accept these conditions. If for any reason, you do not with to be bound by any or all of the above conditions, you many simply return this book to the publisher for a full refund.

ACKNOWLEDGEMENTS

Once again there are many people I need to thank who offered their support. I don't know if written words can fully express my gratitude.

First of all I would like to thank my wife, Hyeeun. Caring for 4 kids while I wrote this book was not easy. You helped me yet again—thank you!

I also need to thank the people who read the rough copies and offered their feedback. Thanks again to my Mom (Tina Colonnese) for your help with this. And thank you to John Rest, Todd Lavigne, and Stephane Lachapelle for your input and ideas in making the book more user-friendly and interesting.

Thank you.

TABLE OF CONTENTS

*"Without goals,
and plans to reach them,
you are like a ship that has set
sail with no destination."*

Fitzhugh Dodson

Discovering the Secret

*"Information being power, he who has
the information has the power."*
James Lavelle

I retired at 34 a few years ago. The important question is—why was I able to retire so young while most people work into their 60s? How can you also achieve early financial freedom? I've thought about these questions and I've discovered the reason.

If we look back in time, one hundred years ago illiteracy rates were much higher than they are today. You could survive if you couldn't read, but it was a real asset if you were literate. The best professions and the most comfortable lifestyles were monopolized by people who possessed this important tool—literacy. To the illiterate population, reading seemed like such a complex and difficult thing to do—when in reality anyone who has mastered reading knows that is not as difficult as it first appears. Someone simply has to take the time to teach this skill.

In Canada we have made huge gains in literacy, but we offer almost no instruction on how to become *financially* literate. The simple reality is that those who have financial literacy are destined to have a more comfortable lifestyle whereas those who don't have this knowledge are stuck working and worrying for much longer than they need to. Simple financial lessons are not taught in schools. People learn from the financial industry—but most of this information serves the interest of the large financial corporations—not the little investors. The financially illiterate pay huge fees and never really earn enough from their investments to reach financial freedom. That's the secret to why some people will live much more comfortable lives than others without having to work any harder.

Schools are really failing in the sense that they do not teach financial literacy. I remember spending a lot of time on things like "calculating the hypotenuse of a triangle" which was complex and is something I could probably not do today if my life depended on it. In fact I have never been asked to do this calculation outside of my high school exam time. This begs the question of why we force kids to spend so much time developing these tools that are never used by most people in the real world. Contrast that to basic financial knowledge. I have been able to leverage my financial literacy into free time—one of my most precious assets. All our lives are finite and we don't get a dress rehearsal! I retired so early because I had financial literacy—something lacking in many people because we don't take the time to teach it!

There might have been a time where you too learned to calculate the hypotenuse of a triangle or learned some other piece of knowledge that was relegated to the dustbin of your mind never to be retrieved again—as it was not needed. However, if you can spend the same amount of effort and gain financial literacy you will gain freedom. You will use it often just like you use your reading skills on a daily basis. Of course *your life* does not depend on you learning how to invest or understanding the strategies outlined in this book—*but your lifestyle might*! Some parts of this book may be difficult at first, but try going over it a couple of times. Even if the task seems challenging at first, the effort will be richly rewarded. Most people spend years acquiring the skills they need to excel in their careers—and this is a good thing. However, spending just a little more effort learning how to manage your money better can amplify your final results immensely.

An interesting statistic from the 2006 national census showed that the median income for the average worker adjusting for inflation increased from $41,348 in 1980 to only $41,401 in 2005. In other words, over a full 25 years, the net amount the average worker gained was only $1 per week in extra income. The study also found the richest Canadians saw incomes increase by over 16% while the poorest Canadians saw their income decline by over 20% (again adjusting for inflation). I didn't review all the statistics but I'd wager a large part of this gain from the wealthiest Canadians is attributable to company ownership in some form—stock ownership being the easiest way to accomplish this. If you rely *solely* on working for a living, you might find you've hitched your wagon to the wrong strategy or are too dependent on only one avenue. Isn't it better to diversify your income stream?

The strengths of my books have been that they explain investing concepts in plain English. Many readers are turned off by financial books filled with complex concepts and little-known financial jargon. In this book, I've tried to take the various concepts and simplify them as much as possible. Some of the ideas are still somewhat involved, so

I've tried to make things easier by dividing the book into two sections—Basic and Not-so-Basic.

You might have to take your time to read through some of the ideas a couple of times, but overall the information is a lot easier than many high school subjects—and the information should be much more valuable. The effort will be worth it for you. This information will simply make life easier for you—as learning certain skills have always made life more comfortable for those who possess them.

My hope is that my books will demystify investing and allow people to live more comfortable lives. Let's begin our quest by unlocking some of the financial secrets that are preventing you from realizing your dreams.

GETTING VALUE
FROM THIS BOOK

*"Be not afraid of going slowly; be only
afraid of standing still."*
Chinese Proverb

If I would have known about the "Money for Nothing" strategy years ago, I would have retired before
the age of 30 as this information would have
helped me be a much better investor. This book
will help you *lower* your investment risk and *boost*
your returns—a proverbial "free lunch". It is a very
unconventional approach—but so was my strategy
for retiring at such a young age.

My first two books blend together to give you
the tools you need to achieve freedom—freedom
from "wage slavery", freedom from worrying
about your financial future, and freedom to deal
with the financial industry from an enlightened

position rather than *hoping* someone else will manage your life-savings well—a hope that sometimes turns to disappointment.

My three books together are a "financial literacy set". As I've already said, if you gain financial literacy, you will have a much more comfortable life. This book is part of a three book set that will give you the knowledge you need to achieve your dreams faster. Here's the best way to utilize my books (in order):

1. If you have never invested by yourself:

If you have never invested by yourself (or have only had negative investing experiences), you should read *The Lazy Investor* first, which offers a step-by-step guide on how to create an investment strategy that virtually runs on "autopilot". This is the strategy my children are using (without them even knowing it) and they range in age from 1–8 years old. If small children can employ this strategy—anyone can. If you want to invest well with a "set and forget" strategy and you have no investment knowledge and very little money, *The Lazy Investor* is the book to start you on your journey.

2. **If you have already invested, but want to reach financial freedom faster:**

   If you want to see the approach I actually used to retire so early, you should look at *"STOP WORKING: Here's How You Can!"* This strategy includes a look at investing from a Canadian perspective. This is important as many financial books we read are American which makes a huge difference as our companies and investing landscape are quite different. It reveals a strategy that enriches *you* instead of the financial industry and frees you from dependence on the ups and downs of the stock market.

3. **If you want to improve on my original "STOP WORKING" strategy:**

   This book, *"Money For Nothing"* will show you how you can improve on your current investment performance to reach total freedom *sooner* than is typically expected. We will look at ways to avoid overpaying for stocks which will increase your investment success. I'd like to explain the concept of this investing strategy using a fictional example before we get into the specific details.

Suppose your neighbour owns a $200,000 house and he wants to move away in a year's time. He's a little worried that he might not be able to sell his house next year. So you go over to him with a contract which states that you will promise to buy his house for $100,000 next January if he can't sell it to anyone else. For this privilege, you will charge him $10,000 today. He thinks about your offer and agrees— and you go back home $10,000 richer. Whatever happens in a year's time will be good for you. Either you will keep a free $10,000 or you will buy a house worth $200,000 for only $100,000. Either way it's win-win for you!

Now suppose you realize what a great idea this is (for you) so you offer this same deal to many other people in the neighbourhood and 10 people agree to pay you $10,000 today to promise to buy their $200,000 houses within a year's time for only $100,000.

After the year is up, suppose nine out of the ten people you made contracts with sell their houses to other buyers, but one person you made a promise to can't sell their house and forces you to buy their $200,000 house for $100,000. Since you pocketed $10,000 cash from 10 people or a total of $100,000, you would use that money to buy this house—so you essentially get the house for free! Wouldn't this be a great deal for you?

Now back here in the real world you can't do this. *Nobody* is going to pay you $10,000 to promise to buy their $200,000 house for only half that amount. But when it comes to the stock market, irrationality creeps in. You see with houses people simply live there and don't buy and sell daily—they act rationally. But with stocks, every day the stock market bell rings and people furiously buy and sell—often based solely on emotions!

So instead of buying houses at ridiculously cheap prices, this strategy is going to show you how to buy stocks at cheap prices and collect much bigger dividends in the process. These dividends will allow you to earn a regular income without having to work. As a consolation prize, if you can't get stocks at these super cheap prices, you will at least get money for nothing!

LAYING THE GROUNDWORK FOR YOU

"It is impossible for a man to learn what
he thinks he already knows".

Epictetus

My investment strategy was a gradual evolution—slowly changing with the idea of improving and learning from my own mistakes as well as from what other investors had done. Just like the expression that says, "There is a fine line between fishing and just standing on the shore like an idiot", *investing* properly and *speculating* on the stock market seem similar, but are very different. At this point I'd like to dissect my original "Stop Working" strategy and try to explain some of the reasons it worked out pretty well and also point out ways it can be improved for you.

The first idea you must understand is how important your percentage (%) rate of return is.

These are sort of like speed limits to your destination. If you are driving to a destination and it is 200 km away and you drive at 100km/hr, you will reach the destination twice as fast as if you're driving only 50 km/hr. It's the same with investing. If you earn 10% per year you will arrive at your destination much faster than if you're earning only 5% per year. If you can get your portfolio to grow at a faster rate, you will see how your dividend income also grows more quickly. Once your dividend income equals the amount you need to live on, you never have to work for money again. So let's take a quick look at how you can earn more.

The first factor that will help you in your investment success is if your portfolio is invested in partial ownership of companies, in other words— stocks. I don't own any bonds or keep any of my investment portfolio in cash. Jeremy Siegel, a business professor at Wharton Business School, wrote a book entitled, *Stocks for the Long Run* where he analyzed investment data going back to 1802 and he clearly showed the superiority of stocks as a long-term investment. Now analyzing 200 years worth of investment data sounds about as much fun as watching paint dry for most people, but it sure is advantageous to be able to simply take his findings and follow the best strategy using his empirical research. Essentially he found that there are large stock price fluctuations. Stock markets move up and down rapidly and usually unpredictably. However, over time stocks have returned an average of around 10%–11% per year on average since the beginning of the 20th century. Although this doesn't sound like much, it has the effect of doubling your money every 7 years. So if you invested $100,000 and you wanted to retire in approximately 20 years, you could expect your portfolio to double three times and grow in value to $800,000. If your portfolio of dividend-paying stocks is doubling every 7 years, your dividend income should also be doubling every 7 years. So 10% is the simple benchmark for a stock portfolio. If you can invest to outperform this benchmark, you'll shorten your journey to financial freedom.

> *The long-term return on stocks should be around 10%. Any investment you can make that returns you more than 10% is quite respectable and will shorten your journey to financial freedom.*

Bonds on the other hand have returned around 5%. Simply put, stocks are much better long-term investments than bonds (or money in bank accounts) and the difference between stocks giving you around 10% and bonds offering 5% is huge.

Look at the difference:

$100,000 invested @ 10% for 25 years = $1,083,500

$100,000 invested @ 5% for 25 years = $338,635

You earn *almost triple* the profits longer-term by owning stocks instead of bonds. Bonds generally return more than bank accounts, GICs, and other guaranteed investments people often make so any of these "safe" options are going to slow you down.

Bonds, GICs, and bank deposits might be good for shorter time frames, but not great for growing your wealth quickly. Owning too many bonds keeps you in "bondage" or "wage slavery".

To successfully implement the investment strategy I advocate, you simply have to buy great companies that sell products or services you need, then sit and do nothing and collect the dividends. By doing this, the odds are on your side (as 200 years of data shows). However, doing *nothing* is one of the most difficult things for many people to do. You have to have faith in the companies you've invested in and ignore the irrational ups and downs of the stock market.

Even though the stock market acts in a manic depressive fashion, over time stock prices rise with profits and these higher earnings lead to higher dividends (cash being sent to shareholders). Everyone who wants to enjoy total financial freedom should be looking for continuous income and that's what dividends provide.

> *Buy stocks that pay dividends.* *Dividend payments are much more reliable than stock prices. They also let you sleep better if you focus on the cash coming to you rather than the stock market gyrations.*

We'll look at some more information on dividends a little later.

Stated simply, buying and holding stocks longer-term will get you to financial freedom. But how can you get higher rates of return and reach your destination even sooner? If you can learn how to increase your returns, perhaps you can stop needing a paycheque a few years earlier, and free up your time for other pursuits. So how do people do this? Many people feel they can't possibly invest on their own—so they look for ways to invest with the help of others.

Many people turn to "professionals" when investing—such as mutual fund managers or full service stock brokers. If the average investor can't pick the best stocks to buy or the best price to buy these stocks, then the assumption is that a professional stock picker can. Why not hire a broker or use a mutual fund manager to manage your portfolio for you? The thing you must remember is that *nobody* can predict the short-term movements in the stock market. "Professionals" like to give the impression that they have some special powers the rest of us lack, but don't buy into this idea. There is truth to the old quote, "Every day, self-proclaimed stock market experts tell us why the market just went up or down, as if they really knew. So where were they yesterday?"

A number of years ago I was somehow put on a mailing list for a brokerage firm. The brokerage would mail me their ideas and it offered a lot of advice for various stocks. I never invested here, but you might come across someone explaining to you that they have some special research that shows how good they are and how you should invest your money with them. Don't buy into this myth. This reminds me of a story I heard many years ago. I don't know if this is indeed true or not, but it gives an interesting perspective on things…

A long time ago there was a new stockbroker who had just been hired at a prestigious New York brokerage house. The CEO was talking with him briefly and trying to explain to him how he had chosen a terrific career to get into. He took him over to his corner office window and pointed down at the harbour and explained to him that all the yachts there belonged to various successful stockbrokers. If this young fellow worked really hard, he too would someday own one of these impressive yachts.

Then the new recruit turned to the CEO and asked, "Where are all the customers' yachts?"

The CEO could not answer him as he had never seen any. This illustrated who was in fact making money from the stock market shuffle—and who wasn't!

When I hear stories like this I can't help remembering the quote, "Wall Street is the only place where people who drive a Rolls Royce go to in order to get (investment) advice from someone who takes the subway."

Be very cautious when seeking out a broker to help you invest. With this arrangement, the broker is guaranteed to make money—while you, the investor, may or may not make money.

How about mutual funds then? The simple reality is that the majority of mutual funds fail to outperform the stock market. With a mutual fund you have to pay certain expenses which further reduce your returns. It's not uncommon to pay

2–2.5% expenses for some funds. If the mutual fund can't outperform the market—which is not easy—your returns have fallen to only 7.5% (if stocks average around 10% as we saw earlier: (10%–2.5% fees = 7.5%). Once again you will reach your destination later. Please remember that these fees are taken right out of the funds directly, so you don't see this money being taken from you—but it still is. The system is similar to how your income tax is deducted from you paycheque *before* you get your money.

> *Very few mutual funds outperform the stock market. With fees, your long-term returns will probably be lower than 10% and you will reach financial freedom much later. Although fees seem small, they are a huge factor.*

So how can you earn more and retire sooner? Avoid the fees! This will have a huge impact on your financial well-being. Financial literacy gives you the confidence to invest on your own and this is a huge factor whenever you hear about people's investment success.

From experience, I've found that my long-term track investment track record has been quite good, but shorter-term I always seem to pay too much for stocks. I look for good opportunities when certain stocks are being beaten down because of pessimism, but I often buy too soon. This is where I found room for improvement that should help boost your investment returns—the price paid for quality, dividend-paying stocks. If you can buy them cheaper, you will make more money faster—and become financially free sooner!

The prices you pay in buying your shares has a HUGE impact on how well your investment does for you.

Getting stocks at cheaper prices which will increase returns while reducing risk is the focus of this book. It's sort of like an owner of an orchard getting trees to yield more fruit—while investing the same amount of effort. I'll also show you how you might be able to collect some fruit *without even owning any of the trees* (earning money without investing any). This will be done using some tools that are usually deemed risky—but in reality are not using the money for nothing strategy. So first let's take a look at the idea of risk.

Key Points

- stocks have historically returned much more than bonds

- do not just blindly rely on a "professional" to handle your life-savings

- buying quality stocks that pay dividends is very important

- buying stocks at cheap prices will boost your returns

- this book will show you how to lower your risk with stocks and how to buy them more cheaply

Risk (like Beauty)...
is in the Eye
of the Beholder

*"Last year people won more than one
billion dollars playing poker. And casinos
made twenty-seven billion just by being
around those people."*

Samantha Bee

The stock market has been likened to gambling but
it's not—if you approach it in the correct way. For
example, most gambling is a negative sum game
where the odds are stacked against the participants.
In Canada, Lotto 6/49 attracts a tremendous number of people interested in earning quick money for
nothing. The only trouble is that the odds of winning the big prize are almost 14 million to 1! If you
do the calculations for most gambling whether it's
casinos, horse races, or lotteries—the results are the

same. The odds clearly stacked against you. The only consistent "winners" are liars.

That's why stocks are such a better option. Shares represent real companies that produce real products or services and earn income. This income is often passed on to the owners in the form of dividends which was explained in my previous writings. Earnings grow as the economy does. Over the 20th century, the average wealth of citizens of North America grew by 7 times. If you took a time machine back to 1900, you'd find a population where almost 40% of the labour market was engaged in farming—compared to less than 1% today. An infant could expect to live to 47 years old. Cars, telephones, electricity, running water, and a host of other things we take for granted were virtually nonexistent. As wealth has increased, many companies have been able to produce products and services people want—and earn profits by doing so. Therefore by buying shares in companies you are participating in something that grows over time.

So stocks are not the same as "gambling". But what about gambling itself—is that always risky? Mostly it is—but it depends on the perspective in which you're looking at things. If you are Donald Trump—someone who owns a lot of casinos—then gambling doesn't seem risky at all. As the casino owner, the games "of chance" are stacked in his favour. There is nothing "chancy" about them—just simple math which ensures the house wins much more than it loses. Occasional huge wins by patrons, which are reported on whenever someone wins millions of dollars, serve to whet the appetite of other gamblers which brings in even more money.

It's the same with lottery tickets. They are based on simple math designed to separate the math illiterate from their money. There is virtually no risk for the government when it administers lottery tickets—so it's not risky at all—for them!

As mentioned earlier, this book is also going to utilize tactics which are usually deemed to be quite risky, assemble them, and combine them with my original strategy of buying quality, recession-proof stocks with a history of dividend increases to *lower* risk and *increase* returns. The aim here is to use the "money for nothing" strategy to invest and reach financial independence even earlier than you could achieve otherwise. It might contradict some of the ideas you already have about investing. It goes against the standard dogma—but the standard dogma has people retiring well into their 60s! Let's remember to look at things from a different perspective—just like a casino owner does.

Key Points

- the stock market creates wealth over time

- if you buy stocks and hold them, you are like a business owner, and you can reap some of the profits

- risk assessment depends on which perspective you're viewing things from

- the strategy I'll show you will involve using something that is supposed to be risky—but in reality isn't if used as outlined in this book

Using Speculative Markets—To Lower Your Investment Risk!

"If past history was all there was to the game, the richest people would be librarians."
Warren Buffett

I am going to give you a very brief explanation of futures and options—two areas of investing (or more correctly speculating)—one of which we will use later on to reduce risk of stock purchases and possibly create extra income.

A recent book I read was one entitled, *Hot Commodities* by Jim Rogers—who has a pretty impressive investment track record. Written in 2004, he argues that "things" meaning commodities (like metals, agricultural products, oil, etc) are going to go up in price with so many people around the world from China, India, Brazil, etc entering the middle class and having disposable income to spend. As of this writing he has been correct as the price of many commodities including agricultural products have more than doubled. For example, Canada No. 1 grade wheat jumped in price to $798 a tonne from an average price of $252 a tonne the previous two years. Even though I have quite an appetite, I've never bought a "tonne" of wheat, but these prices do affect the cost of the foods we eat. This price rise has mirrored the increases of many other commodities and has caused some food riots in a range of countries from Mexico, Zimbabwe, and Morocco to Yemen, Senegal, and Uzbekistan.

It has not only been food prices that have risen, but the importance of food cannot be overstated. Food price increases have a huge impact on people's lives—especially poor people. Among other commodities, the price of metals has also risen sharply the last number of years—more than doubling in many cases. This has led to some unforeseen events. For example, there was an article in the US where someone in Cleveland had gone around and stolen a number of 188-pound sewer covers to sell for scrap metal. I know Rogers called his book *"Hot Commodities"*, but I don't think he was really thinking about "Hot" commodities—as in stolen sewer covers!

And of course the commodity most of us notice every time we fill up our cars is the price of oil! Oil has climbed relentlessly from around $20 a barrel to over $100! In fact oil affects the price of everything as it is the main commodity needed for modern life. For example, because the price of oil has gone up so much, there has been a shift in crop production from growing crops for food to growing crops to create biofuels such as ethanol.

In his book, Rogers talks about investing in commodities (which we won't get into here) and offers a very good explanation for futures—which has a number of similarities to stocks options (which is what this book will focus on). Futures are basically contracts where you agree to purchase or sell a certain amount of a specific commodity at an agreed upon price at a certain time in the future. Many speculators trade in futures— making and losing huge sums of money in short periods of time as the price of commodities move up and down quickly. It is justifiably deemed a very risky exercise and it is for all these speculators. However, there are certain ways these futures reduce risk for others in the market.

For example, suppose you own a breakfast cereal manufacturer and your products are competitively priced. Most of your costs are pretty stable except for wheat—which is used to produce flour—and also happens to be the largest ingredient of your product. How would a huge price swing from our example above where wheat prices moved from $252 to $798 in about a year affect your costs? How about if the prices tripled again to over $2,000? I don't know specifics as I don't work for a cereal company, but if the costs of one of your biggest inputs rose, it would affect your overall cost of production.

Since it's difficult to pass on these cost increases quickly to consumers by raising your prices without losing sales, your profits can be impacted significantly. Therefore, it actually might *lower* risk for cereal manufacturers to buy some futures contracts in wheat to protect them from sudden price swings. So they might agree to buy 100 tonnes of wheat at the prevailing price, let's say $798 per tonne due in two years. If they did this, they could then conduct business with the cost of wheat being fixed—so they wouldn't be at the mercy of rising wheat prices. By doing this, if the price of wheat did indeed triple to over $2,000 per tonne, they have a contract which guarantees delivery of wheat at $798 per tonne. They have locked in their price.

In this example, we've taken something deemed

"risky" in the form of futures contracts which are traded by market speculators and used it to reduce risk by guaranteeing a price for the needed commodity.

Futures can be used the same way for *producers* of commodities. Farmers have very high fixed costs and if they decide to grow a crop based on a certain price and the price of their crop plummets from the time they plant to the time they harvest, they can lose a lot of money. So by selling futures on their product they guarantee themselves a fixed price before they plant. This form of trading futures would work for a range of companies in various industries including car companies and metal producers, chocolate companies and cocoa producers, etc.

Many speculators buy and sell futures trying to anticipate future price swings. Futures are simply the right to buy a specific commodity within a month and up to two years from the time the contract is made. By entering this world as a trader, one is at the mercy of the market forces and could be forced to buy and sell at the wrong prices. Billions of dollars are made and lost daily in this arena. There are thousands of traders around the world analyzing supply and demand trends and trading these commodities based on their information. I am definitely not smart enough to enter this world—but I am sure smart enough to avoid it. Huge, unpredictable profits and losses are not my idea of investing! I have never speculated in futures as it's too risky. They are beyond the scope of this book. The reason we are looking at futures is to help us understand how they work as they have many similarities with stock options—which is what we will be using to boost our investment performance.

As an aside, I would advise you to never invest in commodities directly because of their volatile nature. If you want to invest in commodities, the safer way is to buy shares in commodity producing companies. For example, my exposure to one of the world's most important commodities and main source of energy required in modern life—oil—has been achieved through my investment in Canadian Oil Sands Trust. Canadian Oil Sands has recoverable resources of an estimated 4.7 billion barrels of oil with a reserve life expected to be up to 60 years of production. Instead of keeping money in the bank (and we know the value of money goes down over time as prices rise) I have "oil in the ground" (and we know the price of oil has risen over time) in the form of partial ownership in Canadian Oil Sands Trust. This is a very long-term view as even though I expect oil prices to be volatile over the years, with 3 billion new potential consumers wanting a North American lifestyle, the overall price trend should be up.

I prefer oil as an investment over other investments such as agricultural commodities for a couple of reasons. With food production, farmers can switch the crops they choose to grow fairly quickly (within a growing season) if prices of a particular commodity rises. In addition, agricultural commodities are grown in fairly stable places such as Canada and the US, so sudden disruptions of supply are highly unlikely. Also marginal land can be brought on-stream with additional irrigation or fertilizer if crop prices warrant—so supply can increase quickly if prices rise. Contrast this to oil, where a huge percentage of production takes place in some of the most unstable places in the world such as parts of Africa and the Middle East. An attack on a pipeline can disrupt the whole system. In addition, crops are grown year after year and production has risen greatly over time with scientific advancements such that the same amount of land has produced more crops per acre. Oil on the other hand is a finite resource whose supply shrinks over time as once you put gas in your car and drive around, that supply has been consumed and is gone forever. These factors that create a dismal outlook for oil consumers are the same factors that make me think having some exposure to oil is a good idea.

Even though we'll never buy commodity futures, this introduction leads to an area that we can use—stock options. As mentioned, by understanding the basic idea behind futures, you will understand options better. Stock options have many similarities to futures contracts. With stock options, you agree to buy or sell certain stocks at specific dates at agreed upon prices. Once again, this area can be very speculative and risky—but here we are going to approach this area the same way the cereal maker from our example above approached buying futures for wheat—as a long-term buyer of stocks.

You are not a cereal producer (and hence a wheat consumer) from the example above. However you are an investor who needs an income to live on. Since you don't want to have to work every day to earn an income, you need assets that generate passive income for you. Instead of doing the 9 to 5 grind 48 or 50 weeks a year, you simply want to walk to your mailbox and pick up dividend cheques sent to you from the companies you've invested in. In *"Stop Working: Here's How You Can!"*

I explained this using an analogy of a fruit tree. You simply want to plant some seeds (buy stocks) and let them produce fruit every year (dividends). You pick the fruit (collect the dividends), but you never sell the trees (stocks)!

The strategy we're going to outline in this book will take it one step further and either allow you to collect more fruit with the same number of trees (buy stocks at cheaper prices and get more dividends) or alternatively, be able to pick the fruit without having to plant the trees (get money for nothing). The whole idea is that the faster you can make money, the faster you can build up a dividend-producing portfolio and hence the faster you can reach financial freedom and no longer have to rely on working for money.

So as an aspiring retiree in contrast to the cereal maker, our production is not cereal, but dividends. Our main input is not wheat, but dividend-paying stocks. Just as the cereal maker buys futures to secure a certain price for wheat, we are going to sell stock options to secure a certain price for our stocks. Just as the cereal maker bought futures (which are deemed to be risky) to lower its risk profile, we are going to sell stock options (which are also deemed to be risky) to lower our risk in stock investing. But before we begin we have to learn the terms. Let's move onto the basic strategy and look at some definitions that must be covered.

Key Points

- companies will buy futures (a contract that locks in a certain price) to reduce their operating risks

- in a similar way, stock investors will sometimes buy options (a contract that locks in a certain price) to reduce their short-term risk

- speculators can make (and lose) lots of money very quickly with options and futures

- we will use options to help us reduce risk and buy stocks more cheaply

Section I

The Basic Strategy...

LEARNING THE LINGO...
AND LOCALE

*"Incomprehensible jargon is the
hallmark of a profession"*
Kingman Brewster

The Lingo

As you embark on your "money for nothing" journey, you're going to come across some words you
might never have heard before. If you have ever
tried to learn a new language, you realize it's not
easy. After 12 years of learning French in school, I
can hardly maintain the most simple of conversa-
tions (but my Korean is a little better). I sometimes
feel my wife is a genius communicating solely in
English despite the fact that her mother tongue is
Korean. With investing, there are also some new
words and ideas to learn, but here I'm going to try

to keep it simple for you. Here's a list of all the new words you'll need to know. There are only 6 terms we'll cover so it shouldn't be too onerous for you. You might want to go over this chapter a couple of times or refer back to it while reading the rest of the book if you come across a term and don't remember the meaning. Here are the terms we'll look at:

1. Options
2. Premium
3. Expiry date
4. Strike price
5. Call option
6. Put option

Options

We are all familiar with what options mean in regular life—this word essentially means "choices". An option for stocks essentially gives the person who "buys" the option a "choice"—the choice to buy or sell a stock at a certain price by a certain date. The buyers are the people we will be selling options to—but we'll look at that a little later. With this strategy we are only going to be selling options and not buying them. So we are going to be offering to buy stocks for really cheap prices—and we will also get paid for doing it—just like the earlier example of receiving $10,000 today for a promise to buy a $200,000 house for $100,000 within a year's time.

Premium

Just as an insurance premium is the money the insurer collects for insuring you, the options premium is the money the option provider (seller) gets for giving the buyer the right to either buy or sell their stocks at a certain price. So we will pocket this money immediately and then simply wait for the prices of the stocks we want to become cheap enough for us to buy them. Again, from the house example, the $10,000 we collect immediately would be considered the premium.

Expiry date

Simply the date the option expires. Options expire the third Friday of every month. So for example, if you buy a Jan 2011 option, it would expire on the third Friday in January of 2011. If options expire without being exercised, they simply cease to exist and the seller of the option has no more obligation to the buyer. This is the same as with lottery tickets. Once the draw has taken place, all the buyers of lottery tickets who chose the wrong numbers simply hold worthless pieces of paper, and the lottery organizer doesn't owe anything more—the lottery organizer has received money for nothing. That's why we'll aim to *sell* options. Think about it—who earns more money over time—those who buy lottery tickets or those who sell them?

Strike Price

This is the price at which you agree to either buy or sell a stock by the specified date. So for example, if you sell an option for the right to sell ABC company stock at $50 by January of next year, the person paying you the premium has the right to sell the stock to you at $50 any time before the third Friday of next January. Again, from the house example, the strike price would be $100,000 (that's the price you agreed to buy the house from your neighbour for).

Call option

This is the right to **buy** shares at a certain price (call = buy) any time before the expiry date. We won't be selling call options. You can read books about selling call options to earn income—but I don't want to follow this idea. Once you have bought the great dividend-earning stocks, you simply want to relax and collect the money on a regular basis. If you started selling call options, you

might lose your stocks—so we will not worry about
call options.

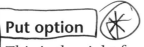

Put option

This is the right for a stock owner to **sell** shares at
a certain price (put = sell) any time before the expiry date of the option. *This is the area we will
focus on and we will only be selling put options
with the "Money for Nothing" strategy in this
book.* This means that the buyers of these options
will be able to force us to buy stock at prices we
wanted to own them at. Just like the example at
the beginning of this book of getting paid $10,000
to agree to buy our neighbour's $200,000 house for
$100,000, we will sell put options (and pocket
money for nothing—the $10,000 in this example)
for the obligation to buy stocks at cheap prices (a
$200,000 house for $100,000 in our example). We'll
expand on this a little later and show how it will be
a win-win situation for you.

The Locale

The next thing you need to know is where options
are traded and how you get the information about
their current prices? In order to use this strategy
and have access to options, you must already have
a discount brokerage account. If you don't have a

brokerage account, you'll need to open one. You can open a discount brokerage account at any of the major banks.

In Canada, options are traded on the Montreal Stock Exchange. To get information on their website go to **www.m-x.ca** and choose your language by going up to the top right-hand corner and clicking on either "English, French, or Chinese". Once you've selected your language of preference, scroll down on the left-hand side and click on "stock options list" under the heading "Quick Links". Then once the new page pops up, scroll down a little and you will see a list of all the stocks in Canada in which you can buy and sell options on. If you click on one of the companies, you will see two boxes side-by-side and within each box a list of different dates and strike prices. The box on the left side is for call options (the right to buy stocks) whereas the box on the right is for put options (the right to sell stocks).

One thing you will notice is that there are long-term options available for some companies but not others—depending on demand. By long-term, I mean they list options for the current year and also each of the next two years. Longer term options are called LEAPS (long-term equity anticipation securities), but you don't specifically need to know this term to make money buy selling them.

Another thing worth mentioning is that the volume of options traded is less than the volume of stocks traded, so you might notice a huge spread (price difference) between what someone is willing to buy options for versus what someone is willing to sell the same option for. I would always enter "limit prices" when placing an order. In other words, type in the price you want to sell your options at, and don't accept the "market price". You can get up-to-the-minute option quotes from your online broker, or you can do this yourself at the brokerage website. You'll have to get someone at your brokerage to explain how their system works and become comfortable with it.

For US stock options, I simply go to Yahoo! Finance and enter the company symbol and then click on "options" on the left-hand side. You will see a list of expiry dates across the top and a box with many strike prices. The top box is for call options whereas the bottom box is for put options. Again, once you've found the information, you'll have to go to your online broker to get the up-to-the-minute quotes and enter your orders.

In dealing with options you are wading into a world you are probably unfamiliar with. Take your time and understand what you are doing before you start actually selling options. I can try to explain the theory of options in this book, but it's difficult to give you all the minute details of the practical step-by-step processes you must do—so use your broker—that's what they get paid to do. Your broker can help you by giving you information and answering your questions as they arise—call them. Another good resource is FREE seminars. I know that TD Waterhouse offers seminars from time to time in various cities on a range of topics (options being one of them). These seminars cost nothing and are open to TD clients and non-clients alike. Simply call TD Waterhouse in your city and ask them if/when they will be having an options seminar and reserve a seat. It's very valuable to have someone in front of you where you can ask questions and get answers on the spot. *You should learn about options before you initiate this strategy. Sign up for some free seminars, read some books on the subject, or talk with your broker.*

Different discount brokers will offer different services, so you can check them out. All the major banks in Canada own discount brokerages, so you can get information by visiting your local bank. However, TD Waterhouse is the largest discount brokerage in Canada, so I will quickly explain how to view options on their website if you have an account with them. If you don't have your account with **TD Waterhouse** then you can skip the next few paragraphs. If you do, you might want to log in and follow this information step-by-step so that you can see how to do it.

Once you've logged in, click on "Options" under "Order Entry" on the left-hand side of the webpage. Then the order page will pop up and you enter the ticker symbol of the stock you are interested in and also enter which market (either Canadian or US). Once you click on "Symbol Lookup" another page will appear. At the bottom left-hand corner under "Options Chain" you enter the ticker symbol once again and also choose the market again (US or Canadian) and select the month you are interested in and click on "Go". A list of all the call and put options for that month will pop up on a screen (call options on the left, put options on the right).

You might notice multiple listings for the same price. This is because you've chosen a certain month but the different entries are for different years. For example, if you chose January as your month, one entry might be for next January and the other entry would be for the following January. (If you are unsure which is which, call your broker and confirm with them).

The fastest way to find out what price the options are currently trading at is to highlight the option you are interested and then press "CTRL" and "C" buttons on your computer (by doing this the computer saves this entry in its memory). Then you simply go back to the main brokerage page and click on "Real-Time Quotes" on the left hand side and then move your cursor to the first empty space and click "CTRL" and "V" and the option information will be entered there. Then again choose your market (US or Canada) and click on "detailed quotes" on the bottom and you will get the current price quotes for that option. You can do this repeatedly for many quotes.

If you can't follow these directions or if you use another discount broker, call them up and ask them to walk you through the process step-by-step. Once you've done it a few times, it's all really quite easy.

Piecing it all Together:

Let's take a look at how all this works out. As mentioned earlier, a call option is the right of the option holder to buy a stock at a certain price by a certain date from the option seller. This stuff is pretty complicated at first so let's look at this idea with an example to help you.

Suppose you want to buy 100 shares in ABC

Inc. and the shares are trading at $50 each. You think the shares should be worth $60 each within a year. If you choose to buy the shares outright, your total cost would be:

$50 per share x 100 shares = $5,000

Suppose you were correct in your thinking and the shares climbed to $60 each within a year. If you sold them, your profit would be:

You sell shares worth: $60 x 100 shares = $6,000
You paid: $50 x 100 shares = ($5,000)
Profit: $1,000

If you sell the shares, you earn a quick $1,000. Here you've made $1,000 profit off a $5,000 investment—or 20% on your money! Of course if the shares had fallen to $40 each and you sold them, you would have lost $1,000.

However, what if you're not sure the price of ABC Inc. will rise or fall over the next year and you don't want to risk $5,000? Here you can buy a call option on ABC Inc. which would give you the right to buy shares at $50 each. You would pay a premium to someone for the right to buy ABC Inc. for $50/share any time over the next year. Suppose the premium is $2.

From this example, you would pay a $2 premium for the $50 call option (option to buy the stock at $50) with an expiry date of January of next year. For this right, ignoring commissions you would pay:

$2 (premium) x 100 shares = $200

In this case, if you are correct and the stock price moves up to $60 you've made a nice profit. Since you have an option to buy the shares for $50, and the stock price is now $60, you can instantly earn:

$60 (current share price) –$50 (your option strike price) = $10 per share

If you do this, you've earned ($60–$50) x 100 shares =$1,000 profit

Since you only paid $200 ($2 x 100 shares) for the options, you earned:

$1,000 (profit from shares) –$200 (cost of call option) = $800

So you've made $800 profit on an initial investment of only $200—or you've made a stunning 400% in less than a year! This is why so many speculators flock to the options market like land speculators flocked to areas where gold rushes took place—the possibility of quick money! It's interesting to note how lottery speculators line up to buy tickets whenever jackpots climb—a little gold rush mentality still exists.

Now from our example above, suppose again you pay the $2 premium ($200 total) for the call option (right to buy the stock) at $50, but instead of rising to $60, the stock price remains constant (or declines). In this case, you would not exercise the option and it would simply expire worthless. The person who sold you the option would pocket your $200 and you would be left with nothing— sort of like having the wrong numbers after the winning numbers have been called for the lottery. You are left with a worthless piece of paper in this case. However, you've simply lost $200—that's the most you can lose. If you had bought the stock, you could lose up to $5,000.

However, how often do people buy the winning lottery ticket? How often do they buy a losing ticket? For your own financial well-being, think of options the same way—never *buy* options—only *sell* them!

Remember, the vast majority of options expire worthless. I have never bought any options and I never will. When options expire, the buyer of options has *paid* money for nothing whereas the seller of options has *received* money for nothing. Remember:

Most options end up expiring worthless. When this happens, options sellers get "money for nothing" whereas options buyers get "nothing for money". What sounds like a better deal to you?

Remember, your ultimate goal is to buy superior quality stocks and simply collect the ever-rising dividends. Stocks are great long-term investments because the profits (and hence the dividends) rise over time as the economy grows. Time is the friend of the investor who buys quality companies and holds on to them. Investing can be win-win for everyone as the value of great companies rise over time.

With options in contrast, the total amount of money earned is *less* than the total amount of money invested (or more accurately gambled) because for every winner (who gains on the option) there is a loser (who loses an equal amount of money). But there are also brokerage commissions and taxes to be paid. The final result is that options are generally a negative sum game—just like casinos and lotteries.

To make money" trading" options, you have to be smarter than the next guy—which is easier said than done. DON'T try to "trade" options for profit as it's a negative sum game—it's only a "sure thing" for brokers who earn commissions and the taxman who collects more income tax.

Here we are not "trading" options. We are only selling options on stocks that we want to own with the ultimate goal of getting to buy the stocks cheaply. The next chapter will show you how the strategy in this book creates a "heads" you win, "tails" you also win situation.

"Putting" the "Money for Nothing" Strategy to Work ... so YOU Don't Have To!

"If inflation continues to soar, you're going to have to work like a dog just to live like one."
George Gobel

Now that you have a basic understanding of options and realize why options are *generally not* a great value for investors, we're going to expand on the very simple strategy which can enhance your returns and help you reach financial freedom sooner. We are not going to get into the complexities of a multitude of options strategies as generally I don't think options are great for long-term investors as explained in the last chapter. With this strategy, I'm attempting to simply reduce your risk and increase your investment success *with the ulti-mate goal of buying great stocks that pay dividends!*

At the time of this writing there is pessimism surrounding some of the Canadian banks because a lot of US banks have done some really dumb lending—such as lending to people who can never repay their loans. Over the last number of years as housing prices rose south of the border, people would refinance their mortgages and borrow more.

For example, suppose someone originally had a $200,000 mortgage on their $225,000 house. As the housing market was robust, over a few years their house might have risen in value to $325,000. Instead of simply being happy that their house had gone up in value and continuing to pay down their mortgage, many Americans would go back to the bank and borrow more money—let's say an additional $100,000 and use this money to buy a boat, SUV, some new furniture, and perhaps a nice vacation. Now that the economy is slowing in the US, many people don't have the money to pay off these mortgages. As John Paul Getty once said, "If you owe the bank $100 that's your problem. If you owe the bank $100 million, that's the bank's problem." There are billions of dollars owed and it is definitely the banks' problem—as many people now owe more on their houses than the houses are worth. Many borrowers will simply hand over their keys and walk away. Banks have done stupid things before—and now they've done it again. John Stumpf (CEO of Wells Fargo Bank) had the best quote on this when he said,"Why invent new ways to lose money when the old ones were working so well."

Canadian banks have done dumb things before too and in this case a few of them also participated in this silliness. However, lending in Canada has been much more conservative and this problem won't hugely affect most of the Canadian banks. Regardless, bank shares have moved down in price as pessimism has crept into the stock market. Usually I would take this opportunity to move in and buy bank shares. Let's look at this using Scotiabank as an example using figures at the time of this writing:

Current Share Price : $48.00/share
Dividends per Share: $1.88/share

At the time of this writing you can buy shares in Scotiabank, which has a great history of dividend increases for $48 per share and get:

$1.88 (dividend) divided by $48 (share price)
= 3.9%

You can get a 3.9% dividend and this should grow over time as history has shown. If you bought shares at the current price, here's what it would look like:

500 (shares) x $48 (price/share) = $24,000
Which earns you:
(1.88 per share x 500 shares) = $940 per year

If you follow the traditional stock-buying approach, you could invest $24,000 and start earning $940 every year immediately.

In contrast, let's look at the "Money for Nothing Strategy" outlined in this book instead. Right now (April 2008) you can sell put options on Scotiabank with the following details:

Strike Price:	$48.00
Expiry Date:	Jan 2009
Premium:	$4.15/share

Suppose instead of buying 500 shares directly, you sell 500 put options as shown above. Here you are giving the buyer of the option the right to sell you his shares in Scotiabank anytime before the 3rd Friday in January 2009 for $48 each. I like to call this a "heads you win", tails you also win" situation because either you earn money for nothing or you buy the shares that you wanted to buy for a cheaper price. Let's look at the *only* two possible outcomes of employing this strategy:

1. You don't buy the shares (price stays above $48 per share):

You sell 5 contracts (representing 500 shares as one contract equals 100 shares) for $4.15 per share. The stock price stays above $48 per share and you are never forced to buy the shares. Ignoring commissions for simplicity, you'd earn a *free*:

500 shares x $4.15 (premium per share)
= $2,075

In this case, a little over $2,000 simply gets deposited in your account—this is your money for nothing! After the 3rd Friday in January 2009, the option expires worthless and you have no obligation to buy the stock.

2. You are forced to buy the shares (price moves below $48 per share):

As shown above, you've sold 5 contracts (representing 500 shares) for $4.15 each, so you immediately gain $2,075.

The share price moves below $48 and the buyer of the put option forces you to buy the shares—shares you wanted to buy at $48 anyway!

Here's how it would look:

$48 x 500 shares:	$24,000
Less premium:	($2,075)
Total Cost:	$21,950

($21,950 divided by 500 shares)
= $43.90 per share

Since you pocketed the premium, your cost per share falls to $43.90 per share instead of $48 you were originally going to pay.

Since you only paid $43.90 per share, your dividend rate is:

($1.88 divided by $43.90) = 4.3% (instead of 3.9% above)

This brings us to the point of this chapter:

By selling put options (which might force you to buy the shares at the same price you wanted to buy them anyhow), instead of buying the shares directly, one of two things happen (and they're both good):

① You get the shares for a cheaper price, or

2.

You earn money without having to invest any— money for nothing!

If it's Win-Win for Option Sellers, Who's Buying and Why?

You might ask why someone would buy these put options. Remember I mentioned that most options expire worthless and you should never buy options. The difference is who's doing what. It's my assertion that investors might sell put options in certain circumstances to try to get stocks at cheaper prices, but only *speculators* buy options— those hoping for quick gains.

From the example above, suppose Scotiabank shares drop to a price of $42/share within a year. If someone had purchased the options that you sold above (for $4.15 per share), he could now buy the shares for $42 and immediately sell them for $48—for a profit of $6.00 per share. Here's how it would look:

He earned: $6.00/share x 500 shares = $3,000
He paid: $4.15/share x 500 shares = $2,075
His profit: $ 925

In the above example, the investor earned $925 on an initial investment of $2,075. So he would earn ($925 divided by $2075) = almost 45% in only nine months! Quick gains like this lure in speculators who see the potential for easy money. But more often than not, the options simply expire worthless. This is the lottery ticket approach to options and that's why I never buy options, I only sell them— and only on stocks that I would like to own anyway.

However, what if the price of this stock does fall back to $42/share? How does this affect you, the option seller?

You sold options at a strike price of $48 and now own shares only worth $42. Remember my dividend-based strategy ignores the ups and downs of stock prices. These random stock price movements are only "noise" in the short-term and are not important for long-term dividend-collecting investors. However, let's look at what happens from a short-term perspective to see how selling put options not only *increases potential profit but also decreases short-term risk*. Let's do this by comparing buying the stock outright versus selling the put option.

1. If you buy the shares at $48 each and they fall to $42 each:

You Paid: $48/share x 500 shares = $24,000
Current Value: $42/share x 500 shares = $21,000
Current Losses: ($3,000)

By buying the shares outright, you've lost $3,000 or 12.5% of your investment from a *short-term perspective.* Just to reiterate, I would simply hold these quality shares and collect the dividends, so this price drop would be insignificant.

2. Sell put options (at $48) on the shares:

By selling put options you've gained the premium:

$4.15/share premium x 500 shares = $2,075

Since you earned $2,075 by selling options, even though you lost $3,000 because the stock price dropped (from above), your total loss is reduced to:

($3,000 − $2,075) = $925

So under this scenario, a short-term "loss" of $3,000 from buying the shares directly is reduced to only a $925 "loss" by selling put options.

By selling "risky" put options, you not only increase the likelihood of better returns, but also reduce your risk.

You can see how options might help improve your returns and also lower your risk. The next chapter is going to look at an easy way of investing where you don't have to decide which stocks to buy and what prices to pay. I'll show you how to get someone else to pick your stocks for you. It's going to show you how to benefit from the knowledge of expert stock pickers—without having to pay any fees!

Key Points

- buying quality stocks and holding on is a great investment approach

- buying when stock prices are cheap improves your returns

- if you sell put options—2 possible outcomes can occur and both of them are good for you

- if you don't have to buy the shares you sold options on, you pocket free money

- if you do buy the shares you sold options on, you get the shares at really cheap prices

THE LAZY "MONEY FOR NOTHING" INVESTOR'S STRATEGY

*"Imitation is the
sincerest form of flattery"*
Charles Colton

Let's look at a "lazy way" to implement this strategy so that you don't have to research which stocks to buy. Here's a very simple way that could prove effective. Let's use a fictional example to explain how this will work.

Suppose there are students writing their final exam for a course. Many of them are relatively confident in their ability to do fairly well—but there are the elite students who want to get nothing less than perfect and there are the lazy students who hope to just squeak through with a passing grade.

They all arrive and are ready to go. Then the instructions are given and they realize that this is going to be a very unconventional exam situation. The rules are explained and they include the idea that everyone taking the exam will answer all the questions they can on their own. Then during the last hour everyone must leave their answers open for inspection from any of the other students. The students can all walk around and simply copy any student's answers before submitting their own exams. There is no concept called "cheating"—it's more looked upon as "creative research".

In this scenario there would be the few diligent or exceptionally bright students who had studied really hard and they would read the exam questions and answer them in an almost flawless fashion. Then the other lazy students would go around and copy all the best answers. The final result would be that even the laziest of students who missed the entire semester of classes would earn a grade as high as the best students as they feverishly used that final hour to copy the best answers. This system might not seem fair, but that's how this situation would all play out.

How does this relate to investing? Well with the advent of the internet, there is an incredible amount of information available. With the many laws passed by securities commissions forcing transparency, many of the best investors have to reveal their stock picks at certain times. When this information is provided, you can see which stocks and the approximate stock prices expert investors have invested in. For example, if I wanted to know what stocks Warren Buffett had purchased recently, I would simply Google "Warren Buffet stock picks". There is also a list of recent stock purchases made by all the best investors at the website **www.gurufocus.com**. Using this site you simply have to figure out who the smartest investors are and then use this information to help guide your stock picks. The only downside is that this information is mostly for US investments—so it can be a good strategy for the US portion of your portfolio. For Canadian investments, this information is often available from mutual funds in their quarterly reports or prospectuses—sometimes available online. You can get ideas from these reports and use this information without incurring the associated fees.

Personally, I don't like to blindly follow what others are investing in, but if there are some super investors you follow, couldn't you simply sell put options on the same stocks they bought? You could set the strike price for the same prices they paid. If you did this you would either earn free money or you would end up buying stocks that the super investors had researched and decided were good buys for a cheaper price than they got them for! This is the ultimate lazy investor strategy and it's a simple way for a copy cat to become a fat cat.

The next chapter will show you how to earn over 10% by keeping your money in a bank account.

Key Points

- you can copy great investors and reap good returns

- certain investors are required by law to reveal their stock purchases periodically

- by selling put options on what they bought, you can either get the same stocks they did for similar prices or earn money for nothing

Bank Account Paying 10–12% or Buying Stocks on Sale!

"A bank is a place that will lend you money if you can prove that you don't need it."

Bob Hope

Across Canada, millions of Canadians keep their money in bank accounts earning less than a meager 1%. There are some who find non-traditional bank accounts and earn between 3–4%, but not much more. At that rate people are actually losing wealth as their money is not even keeping up with inflation and taxation. Using the strategy explained in this chapter, you'll see how you can keep your money in a bank account and still earn around 10–12%.

I am going to show you (with real-life figures at the time of this writing) the actual options I sold to explain how anyone could have structured this strategy. This is a real example of the "heads you win, tails you also win" idea. As before, the "heads" will represent the idea that you sell options and collect the premium, but are never forced to buy the shares. The "tails" will represent the idea that you are forced to buy the shares at the strike price. This is similar to what I went over in previous chapters with a slight difference as the interest earned from money in the bank will be shown.

In early 2008, a search of the internet found that PC Financial offered a savings account that paid 3.85%. PC Financial is a bank operated by CIBC which is a member of the Canadian Deposit Insurance Corporation. This means that if you deposit money into an account, you are totally protected up to $100,000 in the unlikely event that the bank should fail. So by depositing your money into a savings account similar to this, you could have earned 3.85% guaranteed. In addition, you are not locking your money in—you can withdraw your money at any time if you need it.

At this point you should be aware of the other possible guaranteed investments that you could have chosen for your money during this time. You could have locked your money into a 2-year GIC at 4% (or by locking in your money to a 5-year GIC you could have earned 4.2%). You could have chosen a bond—but the rates varied from 3.5% to 3.8%. So by choosing any of the regular "safe" investment options, the best any investor could have achieved was around 4.2%.

At that rate, your wealth would have been hardly growing faster than inflation. So here's a strategy that would have allowed you to earn 10-12% using our "money for nothing" strategy.

The first step involves opening a regular savings account with PC Financial. To do this, you simply go to www.pcfinancial.ca. When the webpage comes up, click on "apply now" on the right-hand side near the top of the page. Once a new page appears, click on "how to apply" near the bottom. Once the new page appears, you will see a few different ways to apply for your own PC Financial bank account. At the time of this writing, by depositing your money in a savings account, you would have earned a guaranteed 3.85%.

The second part of the strategy involves selling put options on a dividend-paying company you'd like to own shares in. Here is an article I wrote in *"The Canadian Moneysaver"* magazine **www.canadianmoney saver.ca**. about Bank of America in mid-2007:

Sub prime Becoming Prime Time!

"A banker is a fellow who lends you his umbrella when the sun is shining, but wants it back the minute it begins to rain."
Mark Twain

It's beginning to "rain"! Headline after headline has been exclaiming the growing credit crunch and the sub prime worries in the US. Concern has been spreading about how this is going to affect the economy and by extension the stock markets, not only in the US but also here in Canada, and abroad.

Sub prime lending (which involves lending to higher risk borrowers) gathered steam in the US over the last number of years within an environment of low interest rates and a strong housing market. Essentially, many people borrowed more money than they could afford. As these borrowers default on their payments, banks will be forced to make provisions for bad debts and reduce their lending, which will reduce liquidity (the amount of money in the economy).

So what's an investor to do under this scenario? Should we be running for cover? Where is a safe haven?

Now I am no financial analyst, but here's my thinking. I like trouble (in the financial world) *because it creates pessimism. I like pessimism because it lowers people's expectations. With investing, as expectations are lowered, so are share prices. This is the sort of environment which presents opportunities. The best opportunities might be in investments closest to the trouble ie. "ground zero", of the sub prime meltdown. This leads me to consider US financial companies.*

The key here is to find companies that have become beaten down because of "guilt by association". I don't want to put my money into a financial institution that is destined for bankruptcy because of stupid lending practices, but I would like to find a company whose stock price has been beaten down simply because they are in the business of lending money (but whose overall exposure to all this is small). I think that I've found one in Band of America—and I recently bought some shares.

Bank of America is huge. It is the largest commercial bank in terms of deposits and the largest company (by market cap) not included in the Dow Jones Industrial Average. It is also a leading participant in the credit card industry with its acquisition in 2006 of MBNA. With a market cap of over $200 billion, this is a massive financial company. This company will *probably still exist when your grandchildren are ready to open their first bank account.*

If you've ever traveled through the US, one of the things you notice is that the banking industry is much more fragmented than here in Canada where our banks form an oligopoly. But this has been changing as US banks merge and grow. The history of successful acquisitions with Bank of America is extensive. Acquisition-related cost savings can be a huge benefit for many financial companies, which is one of the reasons banks in Canada have been seeking approval from the federal government to merge since the 1990s. In the US, consolidation has been going on for a long time. With Bank of America being so successful, if its intended acquisition of LaSalle Bank for $21 billion goes through later this year, it will put Bank of America right around the 10% mandated limit imposed by the federal government of total bank deposits in the country (there has been some talk of lobby efforts to get this limit increased).

The advantage of this size is stability—larger banks are much less likely to fail than smaller ones and Bank of America s very stable. In addition, it has over 5,700 branches and 17,000 ATMs, making it convenient for its customers to access cash anywhere in the country without incurring additional fees. The combination of greater convenience and safety helps attract more customers over time.

Earnings have increased almost 10% per year for the last 10 years with projected 9% growth over the next few years. Although this growth rate is nothing to get excited about, when you combine it with the relatively cheap share price (especially for Canadians since the Loonie is trading near generation highs versus the Greenback) and a generous yield of over 5%, you can see a solid, relatively low-risk return over the long term.

Since this is a US company, you will have to pay a 15% withholding tax on any dividend income. Regardless, even with this reduction, your payment will still amount to 4.5%—a pretty generous initial payout. Just as a farmer buys hens for eggs, I feel investors should buy stocks to get dividends. In fact it's dividends that paid for my retirement at 34! Three years into retirement I've seen my dividend income climb relentlessly higher (faster than the rate of inflation).

In my newly published book, The Lazy Investor, *I continue with the emphasis on dividends (combined with DRIPs and SPPs). However, I ratchet up my criteria for dividend growth from*

*mere "High Dividend Achievers" (at least 10 con-
secutive years of dividend growth) to "Dividend
Aristocrats" (at least 25 years of dividend
growth). Out of the thousands of publicly traded
companies in the US, only 58 make this elite list.
One of these stellar performers is Bank of America with 30 consecutive years of dividend increases. In July 2007, the dividend was hiked
once again, by 14%. This regularly increasing
cash payment, which arrives regardless of how
much pessimism grips the stock markets, has
risen more than three-fold over the last 10 years—
a steady advance. In fact I only own four dividend-paying US stocks and all of them are on the
aristocrats' list.*

*So that is my mind-numbingly boring, repet-
itive, yet very effective strategy. Seek out companies which are being beaten up because of the
short-term issues surrounding the market. Make
sure they are dominant in their industry and have
a long history of paying out increasing dividends.
Then sit back and ignore the hysterics, and keep
collecting your ever-increasing dividends.*

At the time of this writing I was thoroughly
convinced that Bank of America was a great long-

term hold and I still like the company. Shorter-term, with a shaky US economy, the stock price could move down significantly more. However, this company will benefit once the economy recovers. In fact recessions are often a gift to stronger companies as they gain market share when weaker firms disappear. So here's what you could have done using this example (I will use the exact real-life figures when I sold options in this company).

At the time of my put option sale, Bank of America shares were trading between $40 -$45 per share. I felt that the shares offered reasonable value at that price, but I wanted them cheaper. Therefore I sold put options with a strike price of $35 and more put options with a strike price of $30. The option premiums I received for this was $4.90 for the $35 strike price and $3.20 for the $30 strike price. I sold 5 contracts (representing 500 shares) at each strike price. Here's a breakdown:

500 put options x $4.90 each =	$2,450
(Jan 2010 expiry, $35 strike price)	
500 put options x $3.20 each =	$1,600
(Jan 2010 expiry, $30 strike price)	
Total money received	$4,050

For the free $4,050, I sold put options (gave the buyer of the options the right to sell the shares) at $35 and $30 each. If the share prices fell, here is the breakdown of my total possible financial obligation:

500 shares x $ 35 each =	$17,500
500 shares x $30 each =	$15,000
Total possible cost of shares:	$32,500
Less: Premiums received	($4,050)
Total Possible Obligation	$28,450

For the sake of simplicity, these calculations ignore the Can/US dollar exchange rates (which were close to parity at the time of this transaction). So here's how the whole strategy would fit together if you were following it.

10–12% "Bank Account"

You would take $28,450 (of your own money) and deposit it into a simple PC Financial savings account earning 3.85% (as mentioned earlier).

Next, you would sell the put options with strike prices of $35 and $30 (from our example above) and deposit this additional $4,050 premium into your bank account (remember you receive your options premium immediately). Now you would have a total of $32,500 in your savings account.

This amount would cover the total possible cost of the shares. Since you received $4,050 in options premium and these options expired in two years, you would earn:

$4,050 divided by 2 years = **$2,025 per year**
(in options premium)

Meanwhile, your $32,500 in the savings account would earn:

$32,500 x 3.85% = **$1,251 per year**
(in interest)

So the total amount you would earn per year would be:

Options Premiums per year	$2,025
Interest per year	$1,251
Total Earnings (per year)	$3,276

Since you are only investing $28,450 of your own money, you would earn:

$3,276 divided by $28,450 = **11.5% per year on your money!**

You earn this by keeping your money in the bank! If you never buy these stocks, you simply keep this money.

You can sometimes earn 10–12% (more than the approximate long-term average return for stocks) without having to actually own the stocks.

If You Have to Buy the Stocks on Sale

The second possible scenario is if the stock price declines and you are forced to buy the shares at the strike price. What happens then?

At the time I sold these options, I felt Bank of America would be a great long-term investment with its 30-year history of increasing dividends. I wanted to own this company. By selling put options, I might be able to purchase the shares very cheaply if the options were exercised. Here are the possible prices:

Strike Prices	$35.00	$30.00
Less: Options Premiums	($4.90)	($3.20)
Stock prices using options	$30.10/ share	$26.80/ share

At the time I wanted to buy this company, the shares were selling for around $42. You can see that by selling the put options, if I do end up buying the shares, the price I get them for will average around $28—a pretty sizeable discount.

If I had bought them at $42 per share, my dividend income would have been:

$2.56 (dividend) divided by $42 (share price) = **6.1% per year**

However, if the options are exercised at my strike prices, I will buy them for $30.10 or $26.80 each. In this situation, my dividend income will be:

$2.56 (dividend) divided by $30.10 (share price) = **8.5% per year**

$2.56 (dividend) divided by $26.80 (share price) = **9.6% per year**

> *By selling put options, you can sometimes get shares of dividend-paying stocks at much cheaper prices. By doing this your dividend income becomes much larger.*

The next section is going to look at other strategies that are a little more involved but also potentially quite rewarding.

Key Points

- by keeping your money in the bank and selling options, you can sometimes earn fairly high returns of 10% or more

- if you are forced to buy the shares you sold options on, you will get the shares at really good prices

- by buying the stocks cheaper, your dividends become larger

- either way, the outcome is good for you

Section II

Not-so-Basic Strategies

GETTING RICH—WITH OTHER PEOPLE'S MONEY!

"There's only one thing I like more than money—other people's money"
Lawrence Garfield
(from the movie *Other People's Money*)

One of the factors that I employed to retire very early was to use the bank's money to make more money for myself—borrowing to invest. This strategy, known as "leveraging", is *not necessary* to reach financial freedom—but it can speed up the journey. Many people argue this strategy is "too risky" and I would agree that it is not for everyone, but if you do it right, it can be a powerful tool. Think about it for a moment. Banks have been great investments for longer than most people have been alive, but their primary method of earning money involves paying savers a certain rate of interest and lending that money out at a higher rate of interest.

People borrow hundreds of thousands of dollars to buy a house without thinking twice about it—but borrowing money for investing is deemed risky. Even though I don't advocate this idea for novice investors, I'd like to use this chapter to explain how I used leverage to reach my goals earlier and offer some guidelines for those who do want to consider using leverage to earn more investment income.

To see how I borrowed money to make money, we have to go back to the height of the "dot-com" mania when everything internet-related was going up like crazy. Computer-savvy twenty-somethings were becoming overnight millionaires as they developed internet sites that appealed to "investors' (I'd say speculators), and internet-related stock prices shot up towards insanity. Stocks were the place to be—or more accurately, computer-related stocks! Portfolios were jumping 100% and more in a matter of months and everyone who invested in stocks was getting rich... except me!

While the hi-tech frenzy magnified all participants' wealth at a furious pace, I stuck to investing in dull, boring stuff—electricity generators, pipelines, and REITs (real-estate investment trusts). Looking over old investment statements, I see that I bought Riocan in 1999 right around the time I was reading that traditional retailing was a dying business. Riocan is a real estate company that owns a lot of shopping centres and big-box centres that have become so popular over the last number of years. They collect rent from retailers like Wal-Mart, Chapters, Indigo, Zellers, Loblaws, McDonalds, Shoppers Drug Mart, and many others. They then send a large part of this money to investors in the form of distributions (same as dividends) on a regular basis. This is a great business as I've explained in earlier books as once the huge shopping centre is built and all the national or multi-national retailers selling the necessities of life have signed long-term leases, money simply flows to shareholders. There are no possible competing centres as all the land around these centres are used for houses, schools, parks, etc. People simply go there and do their shopping, banking, and dining as it's convenient. So over time, the rents collected go up and the money paid to shareholders goes up.

But back in the late 1990s, there was a perception that people were going to stop going to stores and simply stay huddled in front of their computer screens at home and buy everything they wanted over the internet. Online retailers were going to put traditional retailers such as Wal-Mart out of business. Companies such as Riocan who rented to these "bricks and mortar" retailers were not going to do well and as a result their stock prices became very cheap. I was fully invested at the time which means I had no cash available to invest in Riocan, so I decided to borrow to invest.

In 1999 I borrowed money at 8.5% and invested it into Riocan. I paid $9 per unit and the distribution at that time was $1.04 per share. So the before-tax income from this investment was:

($1.04 divided by $9) = **11.55%**

So by borrowing at 8.5% and earning 11.55%, I was making free money using other people's money (the bank's money—which is how *they* usually make money). In addition, the interest on money borrowed to invest in income-producing investments is *fully tax-deductible*, but the income I earned was partially tax-deferred, so the advantage is even larger. I won't get into a tax analysis of how it was partially tax-deferred because it is beyond the scope of this book, but understand that some REITs offer certain tax advantages and Riocan was one of these.

Fast-forward 9 years or so to the time of this

writing and Riocan's distribution has grown to $1.35 per share which works out to a 15% annual cash distribution based on my original purchase price of $9. This is to be expected. What was your house worth in 1999? Has the price gone up? Shouldn't commercial real estate prices also go up over time? If commercial real estate prices go up over time, wouldn't rents also increase just as the cost of renting a house goes up over time? If rents are rising, wouldn't companies like Riocan earn more profits and use this extra money to raise their distributions to shareholders?

Another example is Pembina Pipelines which I bought for $7.75 per share while it paid $1.05 per share (1.05 divided by 7.75 =) 13.5%. It now pays $1.44 or 18.5% per year based on my original purchase price. Pipelines ship the gas needed to heat our homes and the oil needed to create gas to run our cars—it's essential to modern life. It was a great investment opportunity. Let's take a look at borrowing to invest in this using these real-life prices.

If I borrowed money at 8.5% to buy 1,000 shares of Pembina at the beginning of 2000 and used the income from Pembina dividends to pay the interest on the loan and any extra money left over to pay down the principle of the loan, here's how it would work (in the chart below). We'll ignore the tax effect and commissions for simplicity. Buy 1,000 shares x $7.75 each = $7,750 (so I borrow $7,750 at 8.5%)

An example of the first year figures are shown below:

Earn Distributions: 1000 shares x $1.05= $1,050
Pay Loan Interest: $7,750 x 8.5% =   ($659)
Amount paid toward principle of loan $ 391

** So in 2000, I would earn $1,050 in dividends and my interest costs would be $659, so my balance owing would decrease by the difference— $391 (from $7,750 to $7,359). Look at the yearly results below and see how the dividend income gradually pays off the balance owing on the loan:

Year	Distribution Income (from 1,000 shares)	Loan Interest Cost (at 8.5%)	Balance Owing
Start			$ 7,750
2000	$1,050	$ 659	$7,359
2001	$1,050	$626	$6,935
2002	$1,050	$590	$6,475
2003	$1,050	$551	$5,976
2004	$1,050	$508	$5,434
2005	$1,050	$462	$4,846

2006	$1,140	$412	$4,118
2007	$1,370	$350	$ 3,098
2008	$1,440	$263	$1,921
****Future Projections assuming no more income growth ****			
2009 (est.) $1,440		$164	$ 645
2010 (est.) $1,440		$55	–NIL–

**Notice how Pembina increased it's distributions to shareholders in 2006, 2007, 2008.

So from the chart you can see that $7,750 borrowed in 2000 should be totally paid off by early 2010 *without one cent coming from my own pocket!* The whole loan is paid off by the dividend income. Pembina units currently sell for around $16 each. So *from absolutely nothing,* there now exists an asset worth $16,000 paying an income of $1,440 every year—*forever (and probably increasing)!*

This amount doesn't seem huge but it represents "money for nothing"—no work or effort! This money sort of "appears out of thin air". Suppose an investor had followed the same idea, but instead borrowed $77,500, or ten times as much. He would now have an asset worth $160,000 *generating over $14,000 every year—forever!* He would have created this asset without a single cent coming from his own pocket. How much would a few *free* $160,000 assets help you in realizing your dreams?

I've mentioned that the highway of investing is not a get rich quick idea but more like a gradual process. Leverage allows you to move over to the fast lane and reach your destination sooner. However, caution is essential.

My trip to financial freedom was a learning process and my strategy an evolution. I have used leverage to reach my goals—but I've learned that there is a right way and a wrong way to use it.

A real-life example of "The Wrong Way"

An example of a wrong way was in 1996, when I returned from my year backpacking in Australia. At that time I had been investing on my own for a few years and had been doing pretty well—my portfolio had grown to around $60,000 (which was pretty good for a 26 year-old that only graduated in 1993 and had not yet had a "career job"). I was researching companies and came across Phillip Morris—the maker of Marlboro cigarettes and also the owner of Miller Beer and Kraft Foods.

I am not a fan of smoking—I've never smoked and really hope my kids never do. However I also believe adults should have the right to do it if they want (outlawing alcohol in the US during the

1930s was a disaster). I also don't like the state trampling on an individual's rights. Ethically many people have an aversion to tobacco (and rightly so in many ways), but I don't as long as there are laws which limit the effect on innocent bystanders through second-hand smoke and restrictions on marketing to children.

Regardless, at that time I viewed Phillip Morris as a great investment. This stock idea sounds so stupid to most people—which is precisely what made it such a great investment. The stock was under a huge cloud of pessimism and faced numerous lawsuits which had driven down the stock price to ridiculously low levels. The dividend was very generous and the company had a great track record of increasing these payments over time.

Let's look at some of the positive aspects of this as an investment. The company commands tremendous brand loyalty with huge profit margins. Smokers don't switch from brand to brand like people choose a different restaurant when dining out. Also their earnings rise because the price of their products keeps rising. They don't have to invest in new factories or hire many new people because their sales volume declines by 1-2% every year. This decline is more than offset by price increases. In addition, no new entrants can enter the market as it is next to impossible to win new customers with continually increasing advertising restrictions.

If you read Jeremy Siegel's second book, *"The Future for Investors"* where he's poured over exhaustive amounts of historical statistics going back to 1957, you find that the absolute best investment from the Standard and Poor's index (a list of the 500 largest companies in the US), has been Phillip Morris. In fact it has returned over 17% per years since 1925. To understand how dramatic that is, a mere $1,000 investment in 1925 has grown to over *a quarter of a billion dollars!* What an awesome investment! And all this from an industry that's in terminal decline and shrinks 1-2% per year.

I felt Peter Lynch was talking about this company specifically when he mentioned:

> *"As a place to invest, I'll take a lousy industry over a great industry anytime. In a lousy industry, one that's growing slowly if at all, the weak drop out and the survivors get a bigger share of the market"*

So in 1996, I made one of the riskiest moves in my investing life and decided to invest my entire portfolio into this stock. I then borrowed even more money and invested it. In total I bought almost $200,000 of Phillip Morris (of which around $140,000 was borrowed money). The lawsuits in the US mounted and every day brought more negative headlines. This was one of the most stress-filled times of my life as I had borrowed a huge amount "on margin".

Borrowing on margin basically involves borrowing against the value of your stocks. Anyone owning a portfolio of large stocks can borrow money from their broker solely based on their holdings. They don't have to have a reasonable credit rating and don't need an income or employment history—they can simply borrow money based on the value of their stock holdings. With most large companies you can buy stocks with only 30% down.

So for example, you can buy $100,000 worth of stock with only $30,000 of your own money. So if you choose a stock and it goes up 10%, here's the difference between borrowing and not borrowing:

Borrow 70K and buy 100K of stock	**Only buy 30K of stock**
100K x 10% = $10,000	30K x 10% = $3,000

Here you can earn a stunning $10,000 (by borrowing) even if you only have $30,000 of your own money to invest! In this example, you would earn over 33% on your money by using margin. By simply buying the stock and not borrowing, you only earn $3,000.

However, leverage is a double-edged sword. If you invest in the wrong company you can lose money—lots of it! This highway to financial freedom carries risk. Just as when you're driving down a highway and the posted speed limit is 100km/h, there is a temptation to move over to the fast lane and speed up. If you go 110 or 115km/h, everything should be okay. However, if you want to reach your goal very quickly you might speed up to 130km/h or more. It might work—you might reach your destination much more quickly. Or you might suddenly see flashing lights in your rearview mirror and be forced to pull over and waste precious time (and money).

From our example of borrowing $70,000 and investing $100,000 into stocks, let's assume the investment loses 10%:

Borrow 70K and   **Only buy 30K**
Buy 100K of stock   **of stock**

100K x (–10%) = ($–10,000)   30K x (–10%) = ($3,000)

So here, the "flashing lights" are the fact that you have lost $10,000 of your original $30,000, or a third of your money! Without borrowing you've only lost $3,000 or 10% of your wealth.

If you've bought quality companies that have long operating histories, the 10% decline is probably only temporary. Stock markets are manic-depressive and move up and down like a yo-yo. If you hold on and collect ever-increasing dividends, these setbacks are merely a minor bump on the road to your destination. But if you've borrowed to invest, your broker will call you and tell you that you either have to put more money into your account or they will start selling your shares at this temporary low price. By selling when the price is low, you lock in your losses. In the case above, the value of your portfolio is now only $90,000 (you've lost $10,000 of your own money). Since you need to own 30% of the amount you own in stocks, you need:

$90,000 x 30% = $27,000

But you now only have:

$30,000 (original amount invested) –$10,000 (the 10% loss) = $20,000

So you have to send another $7,000 or your broker will start selling your stocks at this discounted price and the "temporary setback" will become a large "permanent loss".

This is not the worst case. In your effort to move over to the "fast lane", if you've been caught going 150km/h, there are repercussions. In Ontario, if you're caught going 50km/hr over the speed limit, your car can be seized (you don't even reach your destination). From our example above, this is what would happen if the stock you've chosen drops 30%, shown below:

Borrow 70K and buy 100K of stock	**Only buy 30K of stock**
100K x (−30%) = ($30,000)	30K x (−30%) = ($9,000)

Since only 30% of the money is yours, in the borrowed example *you're totally wiped out*. You have no money left! If you had not borrowed money, the 30% decline (which historically is not that uncommon in stocks), would be a painful but probably only temporary setback. You could simply hold on and keep collecting the dividends.

This example reminds me of one of the dumbest things I hear about investing:

Don't believe that if you are young, you can afford to take risks as you have a lot of time to re-

cover. Uncalculated risk-taking is just like betting at a casino—very poverty inducing.

I wouldn't advise anyone to gamble on a "quick roll of the dice". Stick to a gradual accumulation of solid companies with rising dividends. If you want some excitement—take a trip to a casino—but be prepared to have your pockets emptied. If you're young—keep building in a prudent fashion and you'll be free from wage slavery earlier than you think.

So from my real-life example of Phillip Morris, I borrowed a huge amount on margin. As I read the headlines daily, I would stress at the smallest stock price declines. I was totally captive to the ups and downs of the market. I had the gas pedal floored and was simply hoping that I would not get "pulled over."

In less than a year the stock appreciated around 30% and I cashed out. I had managed to double my money—but this was a very lucky outcome. I would not advocate anyone borrow on margin—ever! When you hear stories of people being totally wiped out during the 1929 crash, margin borrowing was the culprit. My investment strategy was a gradual evolution where I learned through a combination of research and making mistakes. This was probably the *only* dumb investing thing I did that had a happy ending for me. So please remember:

Never borrow on margin—it's simply too risky!

You might be wondering why the beginning of this chapter explains the power of gaining wealth off borrowed money and yet it ends with a warning never to borrow on margin. The next chapter will explain a better way to borrow to invest –without all the risk.

Key Points

- borrowing to invest can create wealth for you

- if you borrow to invest, buy quality companies with good dividends

- use the dividends to pay off the loan

- eventually you might own an asset completely free

- *never* borrow on margin

Wealth "Buried" in Your House!

"Take calculated risks. That is quite different from being rash."
General George S. Patton

Houses for many people strike an emotional chord. People love their houses and enjoy them. This chapter might not be for you, but at least read it and see what I'm trying to explain—even if you never follow the idea.

Houses are the largest financial purchase most people ever make. In addition, most people will say that their house was the best investment they've ever made. Buying a house is a huge step towards total financial freedom—a virtual no-brainer. I've heard a few financial-types argue that foregoing home-ownership might be a good move as historically stock prices appreciate faster than houses. While this is true, it's somewhat misleading. With stocks, you can assume a long-term return of around 10-11%. A Canadian study by Remax indicated that houses had appreciated an average of around 5% per year for 25 years starting in 1981. The conclusion some people have drawn is that stocks can be better investments than home-ownership. But this thinking ignores the fact that houses are a place to live—which allows you to avoid paying rent.

A real-life comparison would be the condo townhouse my family lived in a few years ago. It would rent out for around $1,300 per month and it was worth around $200,000. The taxes and condo fees (which covered all exterior maintenance) were around $200 each per month or $400 total. So by owning the house rather than renting we saved: $1,300 (cost to rent) –$400 (taxes/condo fees) = $900 per month or $10,800 per year

If we assume $800 per year in interior maintenance expenses (as all outside maintenance was covered by condo fees), ownership was saving us around $10,000 each year. So as a percentage, we were saving:

$10,000 divided by $200,000 = 5%

We were earning 5% on our $200,000 investment per year by owning the house. If we assume our house would also grow at the average rate from the Remax study of around 5% long-term, our total return was about the same as with stocks—around 10% per year (ignoring income taxes—which further favours home-ownership).

But it is very rare for people to buy a $200,000 house outright. People usually borrow to buy their houses—get a mortgage. So what is your return if you put 10% down (around $20,000) and take a mortgage (current interest rates around 5%) for the other $180,000?

The mortgage costs work out to:
$180,000 x 5% = $9,000

So the savings from owning instead of renting decrease. From above we calculated that you would save around $10,000 (after taxes and condo fees) by avoiding rent. However, if you have to pay $9,000 in mortgage, you are now only saving ($10,000 savings – $9,000 mortgage =) $1,000 per year by buying a house.

So you've made a $20,000 down-payment and you save $1,000 per year by owning the house, so you are *still only earning 5% on your money*! However, you also have to add in the fact that the house appreciates by an average of 5% per year, so ($200,000 x 5% =) $10,000 per year. So by taking your $20,000 and borrowing to buy your house, you've saved $1,000 in rental costs and your investment has risen $10,000, so you've earned:

$1,000 (savings) + $10,000 (price appreciation) = $11,000

So as a percentage, your down-payment has gained:

$11,000 (gain) divided by $20,000 = **55%**

Note that your house has only gained 5% in value with this example. The reason the rate of return seems so high is because you leveraged a lot of money (took out a mortgage) to invest in your house. That's the reason houses are such great investments. You can borrow huge amounts and even though house prices "tick up slowly"; your return is very large because you've only invested a small amount for the down payment. The key here is that there is no fast-moving market for houses. People buy their houses and then ignore minor ups and downs—they simply live there and let the gradual appreciation take effect. They don't get scared and sell in a panic.

In addition, you are required to have the income to support your level of mortgage payments. If you buy a house at a bad time and prices move down a couple percent, the bank doesn't call you and ask you to send extra money to cover the shortfall like they do with margin borrowing as discussed in the last chapter. You simply keep making your mortgage payments and keep living in your house. Eventually the price rises again— it's all very stable.

Eventually you own the whole house. The goal of so many people is to become "mortgage-free"—and that's a very good goal. Once you are mortgage-free, the amount you need to live on is greatly reduced. However, you must realize that once you are mortgage-free, you are earning around 10% from saving on rent and price appreciation combined—similar to the long-term return on stocks. Is there any way to earn more? Can you use your house to safely speed up your journey to retirement?

This next idea is not for everyone, so if you don't feel comfortable with this whole idea, please ignore it. Money decisions are not only financial in nature. You should never do anything that will cause you to stress out and lose sleep.

Never make any financial moves that unduly increases your stress levels—it's simply not worth it!

Having said that, the strategy I'll show you can be very effective. If you are in the financial position to make mortgage payments, once you pay off your mortgage, you have freed up a lot of extra money. Could you not borrow to invest? I am vehemently opposed to margin borrowing, but getting a home equity line of credit to invest is a possibility for some people (if their income can cover the payments) for the following reasons:

1. If they were already making mortgage payments, they could get a line of credit with interest costs for the same amount of their former monthly mortgage payments and their standard of living has not changed.

2. They will not get a "margin call" to add more money to their investments as discussed in the last chapter.

3. Unlike their mortgage payments, money borrowed to invest to produce income is fully tax-deductible which means their actual "out-of-pocket" expenses are less than a mortgage (which is not tax-deductible for your principle residence).

4. Using my dividend approach to investing, you would only buy investments that pay

some form of income in dividends or distributions so this income can be used to make your payments on your line of credit.

Let's take my example from the last chapter—Riocan. Remember this company owns a variety of commercial real estate and it rents to national and multinational companies who offer products and services people need regularly. So in this case instead of borrowing to invest in residential real estate (your house), you are investing in commercial real estate—Riocan.

Assume back in 1999, you borrowed against your home at the rate I did—8.5% (but in reality you probably could have received a much lower rate because loans secured by houses are charged low interest rates). Assume you borrowed $90,000 and bought 10,000 units of Riocan (the same price I bought units for in real life). We'll assume you used the income from Riocan to repay the interest and principle of the loan. Here's the breakdown (ignoring the taxes for simplicity):

You borrowed $90,000 and bought 10,000 shares of Riocan at $9 each.
You used the income from Riocan to pay off the loan.

In 2000 (as shown in the chart below):

You earned $10,712 in income from distribu-
tions (distributions are like dividends)
You paid ($90,000 x 8.5%) = $7,650 in interest
So you paid ($10,712–$7,650 =) $3,062 off
your principle.

** After the first year, your loan balance outstand-
ing falls to:

($90,000 original mortgage –$3,062 amount
paid toward principle) = $86,938
You can see from the chart below that the
loan is gradually paid off each year:

Year	Distribution Income (10,000 shares)	Loan Interest Cost (at 8.5%)	Outstanding Loan Balance
Start	—	—	$ 90,000
2000	$10,712	$ 7,650	$ 86,938
2001	$10,750	$ 7,390	$ 83,578
2002	$11,050	$ 7,104	$ 79,632
2003	$11,400	$ 6,769	$ 75,001
2004	$12,275	$ 6,376	$ 69,102
2005	$12,725	$ 5,874	$ 62,251
2006	$12,975	$ 5,292	$ 54,568
2007	$13,275	$ 4,638	$ 45,931
2008 (est.)	$13,500	$ 3,904	$ 36,335

**** Future Projections assuming no more income growth ****

2009(est.)	$13,500	$ 3,089	$ 25,924
2010(est.)	$13,500	$ 2,204	$ 14,628
2011(est.)	$13,500	$ 1,243	$ 2,371
2012(est.)	$13,500	$ 202	—NIL—

Riocan units are priced at around $20 each at the time of this writing, so if you had borrowed and invested $90,000 in 2000, *you would now own an asset worth $200,000 (with only $36,335 debt remaining). This asset would give you an income of $13,500 every year!* If you did absolutely nothing, your loan would be paid off by early 2012 (or possibly earlier if distributions keep rising as they have in the past).

Think about how powerful this is....you would have created a $200,000 asset giving you regular income of $13,500 per year *without having to spend one cent from your own pocket*—and without really lifting a finger! The income from the asset you invested in paid off the loan you took to buy the investment.

The above example ignores taxes, but by borrowing to invest, you can also save lots in income taxes. Borrowing to invest gives you a tax deduction which has the same effect as making RRSP contributions.

Most people feel that houses are a good long-term investment. If this is true, wouldn't commercial real estate be an equally good long-term investment for the same reasons? Just as houses go up in value over time, so does commercial real estate. Owning shares in a REIT (real estate investment trust) like Riocan is similar to owning a small share of many different buildings across Canada.

This information can be useful for some people who have the income to cover the loan just in case things go wrong—a calculated risk as opposed to being rash (from the quote that started this chapter). Banks have mastered this strategy by borrowing from depositors at meager interest rates and then lending out money at much higher rates. However, I think we can do better. Let's take this idea and move it one step further. How about earning money for nothing from your house *without actually having to borrow any money*? We'll look at this idea in the next chapter.

Key Points

- buying a house is a good investment over time

- the reason houses are often great investments is that people borrow to buy them

- interest on money borrowed to invest is tax-deductible (unlike mortgage interest in Canada)

- borrowing from your house to invest can create a lot of wealth for you

"Renting" out your House: Getting the $$$ without Tenants!

"Becoming wealthy is not a matter of how much you earn, who your parents are, or what you do…it is a matter of managing your money properly."
Noel Whittaker

I love stocks! I love looking at stocks finding great opportunities. I love the fact that I can operate totally independently—contradicting the standard thinking and be proven either right or wrong over time not based on people's opinions but solely based on facts. Entrenched thinking should be questioned—that's how progress is made. I've made many mistakes investing—but I'm happy I went out on a limb and tried things and learned from these mistakes. It's by making mistakes and analyzing what you did wrong that you gain experience.

Borrowing to invest and buying options are both seen as risky endevours, but I feel that both tactics combined carefully can really help accelerate your journey to financial freedom. My investment strategy has argued against the traditional idea of building up a certain fixed sum (the "nest-egg" approach) and instead focused on the income you are earning from your investments in the form of dividends. It's the same way you focus on your income at your job. You simply need to create an income that covers your living costs and ignore the irrational ups and downs of the stock market.

Ah...the irrational stock market. It flies high one day, crashes the next in an unpredictable fashion. It's this irrationality that you can harness and use to your advantage to help create wealth for yourself and move into a position of financial freedom where you're no longer dependent on working to earn money. Longer term the stock market transfers wealth from speculators to true investors.

There are different occurrences that happen from time to time in the stock market that offer great opportunities to make money. The examples sited in the last couple of chapters of Riocan and Pembina Pipelines shows how they became good opportunities when everyone was chasing technology stocks and ignoring the boring but stable industries. There are other times when the whole market crashes—like right after 9/11.

I like pessimism as it beats down stock prices and creates good opportunities to buy cheaply. It seems many investors look for blue skies and sunshine before investing their money. This tends to be counter-productive over time as stock prices are highest when optimism abounds. It's interesting to note that top-performing investments during one year often perform poorly the following year.

Let's use a fictional situation to explain this. Suppose there is a local vendor on a tropical island which receives regular cruise line tourists and he sells only two products—sunglasses and umbrellas. He buys his product from the only place he can get them every day—one central wholesaler. But he can only carry a small amount of inventory at once since he doesn't have a vehicle. So he buys a small amount of one of the two products early every morning and stores it in his hut at the beach. Suppose both he and the wholesaler will raise and lower their prices based on present demand from tourists as a ship brings in only a small amount of product to the island every day (just as stocks move up and down based on current demand from investors). Also suppose that the island has very unpredictable weather patterns (as unpredictable as the short-term movements of the stock market).

In the above scenario, in the morning when the sun is shining and there are no clouds to be seen, umbrellas would sell cheaply and sunglasses would become more expensive. Since he sells these products every day—he would be wiser to buy umbrellas from the wholesaler on this sunny day because their price would be lower (as demand for umbrellas would be very low on sunny mornings). When he gets back to his hut on the beach, he would be selling sunglasses to tourists at high prices. Conversely, when there is thunder and lightening and the rain is pouring down it would actually be in his best interest to increase his stock of sunglasses as the price for them would surely be quite low on stormy days. Here he would be selling the umbrellas he bought cheaply on the previous sunny day. Tourists who are only looking short-term (like speculators) would buy umbrellas on stormy days and sunglasses on sunny days and pay very expensive prices for them. They are only on the island for a short time and need these items while they vacation. So the weather being very unpredictable is a huge advantage for the vendor as he keeps a longer-term perspective. He is able to buy his products at super cheap prices and sell them for expensive prices.

The climate (long-term weather patterns) of the island is pretty consistent. Every year there are many sunny days and many rainy days—so he knows that he will always be able to sell both products over time so he can ignore the short-term weather.

It's the same with stocks as we already looked at. Stocks go through ups and downs as do entire markets—but the long-term shows that great companies that have been in business for years and have increased their dividends for years will weather the storm and do well over time. Those longer-term thinkers who focus on the "climate" will do much better than the short-term thinkers who are only concerned with the "weather". So the best strategy is for you is to buy when the pessimism is at a high—and collect the dividends.

This chapter will combine the ideas of buying when pessimism abounds and look at how you can use the put-selling strategy we covered earlier in the book while using other people's money for wealth creation via a secured line of credit that we looked at in the last chapter.

I'll assume I'm assembling this strategy today— so I'll use today's prices and rates at the time of this writing. These rates will change but similar situations will exist over time.

The first thing I would make sure of is that I could make the payments on the loan if the stock I chose went bankrupt and my investment became as worthless as yesterday's losing lottery ticket. This is very important.

With my strategy, I focus on the highest quality companies that have been in business for decades—or even over a century in many cases. I further reduce risk by focusing on companies that offer recession-proof products or services. To add diversification and reduce risk even more, I invest in a number of companies from a variety of different industries.

So let's take a look at this. Suppose you have finally paid off your house and now you are contributing extra money to your RRSP to save for retirement and also to save a bit on taxes. You have created a plan to contribute $1,000 per month into your RRSP—or $12,000 per year.

Right now (using real-life figures at the time of this writing) you can get a secured line of credit on your house (also known as a home equity line of credit) for up to 75% of the value of your house at prime (currently 4.75%). So if your house is worth $275,000 or more, you can easily have access to

$200,000 in borrowing. To set these up there are usually "fees", but when I got my line of credit, I simply played one bank against the other while negotiating and they waived the appraisal and legal fees. Essentially, *I only pay money if I borrow money in the form of interest.* If I never borrow against it, I never pay a cent.

> *Negotiate with your bank to get all the fees waived if you set up a home equity line of credit. These loans are very low risk for the banks and they like this business, so don't pay them money for nothing—get it set up for free or walk away.*

From the above example, you are already contributing $12,000 per year to an RRSP. However you can borrow $200,000 in which you'd pay:

(4.75% x $200,000) = $9,500 interest.

So instead of investing a full $12,000 in an RRSP, you could borrow $200,000 and pay interest of $9,500 per year. This would reduce the amount you could contribute to your RRSP to ($12,000— $9,500 =) $2,500. Remember, interest paid on money borrowed to earn income is tax-deductible, so the *net tax savings would be the same as contributing the whole $12,000 to an RRSP.*

In reality, if you're following my strategy of buying dividend-paying stocks, you can use the money earned from the dividends to pay the interest on the loan (or most of it) and keep contributing most of the $12,000 to your RRSP. Although you will owe tax on the dividends you receive, dividends from Canadian companies receive favourable tax treatment.

> *You can use the dividends received from the stocks you purchased to pay the interest on the money you borrowed.*

Here's what you would do. Look for great companies with generous dividends that have a long history of dividend increases that are trading at fairly cheap prices. Then sell "deep out of the money" puts (sell put options at prices *much* below the current stock market prices).

Let's go back to Scotiabank that we used in the last section a few chapters ago and use it as an example. Again you would invest in many companies for diversification and risk-reduction, but for simplicity, I'll illustrate this strategy with only Scotiabank.

Here again is the information on Scotiabank:

Share price:	$48 per share
Dividend:	$1.88 per share
($1.88 dividend by $48)	= **3.9%**

You would earn 3.9% in dividend income at the current stock price. However, dividends from Canadian companies get preferential tax treatment. We'll assume in this example that your income is over $74,000 and you live in Ontario. In this case, the dividend tax rate works out to approximately 15%. I won't go into all the calculations to arrive at this figure because it is complicated and beyond the scope of this book. However, if you'd like to see how dividends are taxed compared with regular income, get a free copy of the CGA Personal Tax Planning Guide (which are given away free at most public libraries). There are comparison charts at the back (page 115 in the 2007/08 edition). The net result is that you keep 85% of every dollar earned from dividends (which is why I multiply your dividend by 85% to figure out your after-tax rate). This means your *after-tax* earnings from Scotiabank would be:

3.9% x 85% (% you keep after dividend taxes) = **3.3% after-tax**

Remember that you borrowed at 4.75%, but interest paid to earn income is fully tax-deductible. At the income level we're assuming here, you would be in the 40% tax bracket. This means that for every dollar in interest you paid on your loan, you would receive 40 cents back via tax savings (this is why I multiply your interest by 60% to get the after-tax result). Here is how much interest you would pay after-tax:

4.75% x 60% (after the 40% tax deduction) = **2.85% after-tax**

So even though you are borrowing at 4.75% and only earning 3.9% *before-tax*, *after-tax* you are actually paying only 2.85% out of pocket in interest expenses while earning 3.3% in dividends! So immediately you could start profiting from borrowing to buy Scotiabank shares today.

You might be looking at those numbers and thinking "It's not really worth it to invest to earn a meager half a percent after-tax." I'm simply using Scotiabank as an example—but you could use the RioCan or Pembina examples I used earlier to earn more money immediately. However, bank stocks have generally been great long-term investments. They have rewarded their shareholders with numerous dividend increases. For example, below is a chart of Scotiabank dividend payments for the last 10 years:

Year	Dividends per Share
1998	$0.40
1999	$0.44
2000	$0.50
2001	$0.62
2002	$0.73
2003	$0.84
2004	$1.10
2005	$1.32
2006	$1.50
2007	$1.74

Scotiabank has a long history of dividend increases. For the ten years from 1998 to 2007, the dividend increased from 40 cents to $1.74. In other words it more than quadrupled. From our example of initially earning around a 3.3% after-tax return, if the dividend growth rate continued to grow as it has over the last 10 years, you'd be earning over 14% based on your original purchase price in dividend income within ten years. Again, it's quite possible the dividends could pay off the entire loan and you would have received all the dividend-paying Scotiabank shares without having to put in so much as a cent of your own money (just like we showed with the examples earlier). You would then receive money for nothing in form of dividends for the rest of your life!

> *Dividends receive preferential tax treatment— remember to compute after-tax costs and earnings.*

** Note: The figures above are an estimate for Ontario/Federal combined rates and are only approximate amounts used to explain the general concept. Check your own situation with regard to tax brackets and where you live to make sure you know how everything will impact you before you attempt this sort of strategy. If it is too complex for you, seek the assistance of the appropriate professional.

Buying the shares directly

So if you bought 4,000 shares of Scotiabank outright, your total cost would be:

> 4,000 shares x $48 each = $192,000.
> Your initial cash flow would be:
> 4,000 shares x $1.88 (dividend) = $7,520

From an after-tax perspective

You Earn (after tax): $7,520 x 85%

                 (after dividend taxes) = $6,392

You Pay (Interest):   2.85% x $192,000   = $5,472

     Income per year $ 920

The initial profit is $920 per year—but if your dividends rise (as they have in the past), you will earn more money. As you earn more money, you can keep paying down your loan. As you pay off part of your loan, the interest costs decline. Eventually, just as in previous examples, you could pay the entire loan off and get to keep the shares for free. Again, if the dividends keep growing at the rate they have over the last ten years, within a decade you would be earning *over $27,000 per year in dividend income (instead of the $6,392 shown above).*

As an aside, if the share price increased at the same rate it has over the last ten years, *your $192,000 investment would grow to around $570,000.* So with the dividends paying off the loan, *you would have created an asset worth over half a million dollars without a single penny coming from you.*

What are the risks in such a strategy? For starters, Scotiabank could go bankrupt and you're left with worthless shares and a loan to repay. However, this risk is pretty low as Scotiabank has been around for over 100 years and is a part of the very profitable banking oligopoly we have in Canada. Regardless—low risk is never no-risk and this outcome is *possible.*

Another risk involves the shares going down below what you paid and never recovering. Again based on history this outcome is unlikely.

In addition, Scotiabank could earn less money and cut (or possibly eliminate) its dividend—leaving you on the hook for paying off the loan. Again, Scotia has a history of over 100 years of paying dividends, so the possibility of this happening is remote—but I suppose it could happen.

The previous three possible risks are fairly unlikely to occur, but a risk that has a much higher chance of happening is if interest rates rise and you're forced to make payments on the loan at higher interest rates. This impact would be partially cushioned by the fact that interest paid to earn income is tax deductible, so each 1% rise in interest rates would only result in you paying 0.6% more. However, this is why I recommended only trying this strategy if you already had extra money to cover the loan cost. The example I started with assumed you were already making RRSP contributions and could redirect some of that money towards loan repayment.

Using the "money for nothing" approach

However, let's take this basic scenario and make it less risky. Let's make it so that even if the stock price falls, we'll still be making money! It will have to fall almost 20% before we start to lose money—and only if we sell. Let's also only buy Scotia shares if they can yield more than the 3.9% offered from above—let's say at least 4.75%. How? Simple. Let's only buy them if we can get a cheaper price.

Currently, you can sell a Scotia put option with the following characteristics:

Expiry Date: January 2009
Strike Price: $40
Premium: $1.30

In this case, the stock would have to fall from $48 to $40 in order for you to be forced to buy the shares—or almost 17%. Your cost per share would be:

Strike Price:	$40.00
Less: Premium received:	($1.30)
Cost per share:	$38.70

Since you are now buying the shares for a reduced price of about $38.70, the dividend now works out to:

$1.88 divided by $38.70 = **4.85% before tax**

By selling put options, you've reduced the price you pay for the stock and increased the dividend yield. You can also buy more shares since you are now only offering $40 per share instead of $48 if you bought them immediately. Here are the two possibilities of how the whole scenario would play out.

1. The stock price falls and you buy the shares: Assume you sell put options on 5,000 shares and pocket $1.30 per share. The initial premium you would receive would be:

5,000 shares x $1.30 = $6,500 cash

You would collect this cash immediately. If you are forced to buy the shares:

Cost for shares:	
5,000 shares x $40 each =	$200,000
(less) premium (above)	($ 6,500)
Total cost:	$193,500

So your total investment for 5,000 shares is $193,500 (instead of paying $192,000 for only 4,000 shares from buying the shares directly). Remember, the dividend is $1.88 per share, so your dividend (before-tax) would be:

5,000 share x $1.88 = $9,400

Here's how it would look after-tax:

You Earn (after-tax):

$9,400 x 85% (after dividend taxes) = $7,990

You Pay (Interest): 2.85% x $193,500 = $(5,515)

Income per year $2,475

You are earning an initial $2,475 instead of only $920 in net *after tax* dividend income using the "money for nothing" strategy rather than by buying the shares directly. Again, your dividend income should keep rising, so if you held the shares and used the dividend income to pay off the loan, eventually the entire loan would be paid off. If your dividends grew at the same rate as they have over the last ten years, within a decade your dividend income would be *almost $35,000 per year (instead of the $27,000 you'd be earning by buying the shares directly)*—and you'd earn this money every year forever! Also if the shares increased in value to the same amount as in the direct stock-buying example, in a decade *your shares would be worth over $710,000—and you would have received these shares for free without one cent coming from your own pocket!* Now let's see what happens if you don't get to buy the shares.

2. You never buy the shares:

What happens if the stock price doesn't go down and you don't buy the shares? You simply never have to borrow any money (because you're not forced to buy the shares). If this happens, you simply win the consolation prize and you earn *a free $6,500 for nothing!* What would you do with an extra $6,500 that comes to you absolutely free?

This is like "renting" out your house through getting a home equity loan and collecting $6,500 in rent—but never having to deal with tenants. The next chapter will look at some potential risks and pitfalls of selling options.

Key Points

- you can get a home equity line of credit at very low interest rates

- selling put options on stocks you'd like to own can let you earn money for nothing

- if you are forced to buy the stocks, the dividends can pay off the loan and you get a free income stream

- if you don't buy the shares, you earn money for nothing.

POSSIBLE RISKS
AND PITFALLS

*"You've got to be very careful if you don't
know where you're going, because
you might not get there.*
Yogi Berra

My biggest concern about writing this book is that
people are going to label it as a book about "trading options"—which it's NOT! Generally, I'm not a
huge fan of "trading" anything. Give me a great
stock at a reasonable price that is almost certain
to increase its dividends over time and I'll gladly
tuck it away and hold onto it forever—that is my
preferred method of investing. Options by their
very nature are a bad deal *in most cases* because
for every "winner" there is a corresponding "loser"
—a zero sum game. As brokers collect fees and the
tax department collects their taxes options become

a negative-sum game—just like lottery tickets. In contrast, it is possible that long-term investing can have only winners and no losers—if fees and taxes are kept to a minimum.

> *Generally speaking, options are speculative at best—as they are a negative-sum deal.*

This book is about trying to *invest in stocks* at cheaper prices! The fact is—I am only using put options *as a tool* to accomplish this. My goal is *always* to obtain great stocks at good prices. The fact that I can earn "money for nothing" in some cases if I'm not able to get the stocks at the prices I want is a nice consolation prize—but it is not the aim of the strategy. It is merely free money I receive which pays me to be patient while I keep my eyes on the true prize—great stocks that are going to send me passive income for the rest of my life.

Remember your ultimate goal is to buy stocks at cheaper prices! You are simply making offers to buy stocks at prices you wanted to buy them for anyhow.

Since most people who "trade" in options are speculators, they are deemed to be great risk takers. In fact, when I set up my TD brokerage account to trade options, I had to be approved. They use a level system (from levels 1-4). Level 1 allowed me to buy options as I could only lose the money

I had "invested". Level 2 allowed me to do covered calls—something you can look into if you want, but is beyond the scope of this book and not a strategy I generally pursue. Level 3 was spreads— also beyond this book. Level 4 allowed me to sell puts and calls without owning the shares. This is the level I needed approval for. I had to be approved by verbally displaying that I understood how options worked and the various risks involved. This is a good safeguard for investors and I would be skeptical if your broker didn't make you show that you had knowledge of options before being approved to deal with them—as they *can be* extremely risky.

> *If your broker does not make certain that you know what you are getting into with options, I would quickly find another broker.*

Initially, I was told that I would not be allowed to sell put options as the broker deemed it too risky. I had to explain to them that I was only selling put options on companies that I *wanted to own,* so how was this any more risky than buying the stock outright? It was in fact less risky.

> *The strategy in this book is only dealing with selling put options (allowing someone to sell stocks*

to you) of stocks you want to own at prices you want to buy them at. The overall effect is placing orders to buy quality stocks at certain prices—with the only difference being you get paid to wait.

However, here are some of the risks you might face by starting this strategy.

First, it is very addictive to earn money for nothing. You might be tempted to sell put options on securities you don't really want—simply to collect the premiums. Don't do this! If you start selling put options simply to pocket premiums, you might end up with a portfolio of stocks you don't really want. Also, you might be tempted to sell options at strike prices that are not really very cheap because you pocket more premium money up front the higher the strike price. Again don't do this or you will overpay for your stocks.

Your goal here is to buy great stocks at good prices. The premiums you earn are the consolation prize. Remember this.

Another temptation lies in the fact that most options expire worthless—so as a seller of options you begin to see that you can sell options on more stock than you can really afford—just as airlines often sell more seats than they have available. For example, you might only have $50,000 to invest, but you sell options for $100,000 figuring that most options expire worthless so you won't have to buy the full $100,000 worth of stocks anyhow. By doing this you can make *more* "money for nothing". Remember that stock markets are very unpredictable and your plans can be totally derailed if the markets move against you and you end up being forced to buy more stock than you can afford. There are ways to "close out" positions, but this is beyond the scope of this book and can create losses for you.

> *Just as you shouldn't buy a more expensive house than you can afford, you should not sell options on more stock than you can afford. If you do, you could lose a lot of money.*

One more risk that I've personally taken is in selling US options. If the Canadian dollar were to lose value in relation to the US dollar and I was forced to buy shares in the companies I've sold options on, I would have to spend more Canadian dollars to buy the shares. In this case my cost in Canadian dollars would be higher. This impact is somewhat reduced by the fact that the American companies pay dividends in US dollars, so my income converted back to Canadian dollars would also be higher. However, if you want to avoid any potential currency risk, only deal with Canadian companies when selling put options.

Finally, there are many options strategies out there—and it can be tempting to give them a try. Don't! Stick to what you know and only concentrate on building up your portfolio of great dividend-paying stocks. This book simply offers a method in which to do it by selling put options. Be careful and don't take unnecessary risks.

This is the "money for nothing" strategy in a nutshell. I hope you will find this information helps lower your risk and increases your returns. The following section will answer some questions readers had about my original "stop working" strategy, update the changes I've made to my portfolio since retiring, and give some examples of put options I've sold on stocks I'm hoping to buy.

Section III

My Portfolio
Revisted...

READERS' QUESTIONS ON THE STOP WORKING STRATEGY

"I don't expect anyone just to sit there and agree with me, that's not their job."
Margaret Thatcher

As I already mentioned earlier, when I created my original investment strategy I ignored a lot of the conventional investment "wisdom" and challenged many traditional ideas. I came to the conclusion that a lot of the "advice" out there was created for the benefit of those who provide financial services rather than the consumers of those services, so I decided to create a strategy that would enrich myself (and other investors who followed my strategy) instead of the service providers. I then started my four children on the path to very early financial freedom using a total beginner strategy which also avoided a lot of the usual costs most investors face and avoided to need for an extensive amount of investment knowledge. These two approaches were outlined in my first two books, *STOP WORKING: Here's How You Can!* and *The Lazy Investor*. Thinking "outside the box" and challenging the regular assumptions about investing was the key to the success of my investment strategy.

This idea of questioning everything and not simply following the norm continued with the publication of my books. I rejected the standard approach of using a traditional publisher in favour of creating my own publishing company. Why would I want to give up control? The common practice of using a book distributor was replaced with the idea of doing all the distribution myself. A North American wide toll-free number was created. A website was set up. Total control and responsibility would rest only with me. I wanted a book that was written for the average person—not a complicated 300-page theoretical book loaded with financial jargon—so I sought out advice from non-investors. The feedback I received was extremely helpful in making my book more user-friendly. The final result was that my first two books went on to become National Bestsellers, consistently placing on the top 10 bestseller lists in Canada.

Continually questioning and challenging accepted practices is important and offers a chance to learn. So after publication of my books, I answered e-mails readers sent. I'm open to questions and challenges to my strategy at **www.stopworking.ca** Books are mostly one-way communication, but I've often had a couple of unanswered questions whenever I've read books in the past. I felt if I could offer a chance for readers to question me, then the whole exercise would become more useful.

For the benefit of everyone who has read my books, I decided to include this chapter outlining some of the challenges and questions I've received. You might have had some of the same questions. Hopefully this will help you answer some of those questions...

Your strategy seems overly simplistic. If it's so easy to invest, why aren't more people doing it and becoming financially free?

I've often found that people are attracted to complex solutions to simple problems. I subscribe to the idea of keeping things simple. I've often heard debates where one person takes a logical position and the other person chooses to indirectly attack the argument instead of directly pointing out its actual flaws. This is often because there are no glaring flaws to be found. The detractors resort to mentioning things like, "That's easier said than done" or "That idea is overly simplistic".

Let me restate my position on this—simple is good! There are enough daily challenges to confuse me even on the best of days, so I always choose the least complex solution. A little story will illustrate this. There is some discrepancy about whether it's factual or an urban myth but it is useful as an example of simplicity.

Back in the 1950s and 60s, both the USSR and the US were competing ferociously to become the first country to reach various milestones in their quest for glory and supremacy in outer space. One of the unforeseen problems was the fact that they had to write down their findings for various experiments while in orbit, but ballpoint pens require gravity, so they don't work in space. NASA with its massive budgets set to work and spent millions to develop a pen that could write in a zero-gravity environment—with success!

The Russians, facing much tighter financial constraints never developed a similar pen. In fact they never even tried. Instead they sent their cosmonauts up in space with pencils. It was a simple solution—but still effective.

Investing, like dieting, is really quite simple—

but not easy. It involves sticking with your plan— even if that seems difficult sometimes.

I studied Commerce in university as I figured it would unlock the secrets of business, but when I studied finance I was thoroughly disappointed. There were complex formulae to remember that just didn't seem to make sense to me. I graduated with my degree but I still didn't feel I possessed "the hidden secrets" of great investing. It wasn't until I began reading many investment books from people who had actually amassed incredible track records of investing that I began to realize there are *no complex secrets* to investing at all—only guidelines to follow which help you on your path to financial freedom. By cobbling together a lot of different information from various people, I came away with my nine basic investing tenets that I religiously follow. These tenets are mentioned a little later in this chapter.

The reason most people never achieve total financial freedom is twofold. First, they've never learned the simple investing lessons (less challenging intellectually than completing high school math in my opinion). Second, investing properly requires you to control your emotions and ignore the extreme ups and downs of stocks markets which over time are not as important as they seem.

What if the stock markets crash and your portfolio gets decimated?

The strategies outlined in both the **STOP WORKING** and *The Lazy Investor* rely on dividend payments and ignore the ups and downs of stock prices. The idea is that the stock market is manic depressive in nature, but if the underlying fundamentals of the companies' shares you own are sound, you simply ignore the "noise" and keep collecting the dividends. The idea is to focus on quality companies that offer products or services that are essential (and therefore recession-proof). For example, below is a 10 years of stock data for RBC Financial (Royal Bank of Canada). I've divided the information into smaller sections to help explain some points. Let's take a quick look at the 1997-2007 info in three separate sections:

Year	Year End Share Price	% Change in Share Price Gain/(Loss)	Dividends/ per share	% Change in Dividends/ share
1997	$18.84	—	$0.38	
1998	$17.78	(–5.6%)	$0.44	15.8%
1999	$15.86	(–10.8%)	$0.47	6.8%

By 1999 you have held RBC for a couple of years and the share price has dropped over 16%. Many investors are tempted to sell—waiting patiently and losing money is no fun. But if you focus on the dividends you see gradual progress (and hold on)! The dividends have risen from $0.38 to $0.47 per share—or a respectable 24% in two years. During this time it's interesting to note that many investors were more interested in chasing the hi-tech darlings—any company internet-related, and ignoring the dividend-paying stalwarts like the banks. Let's continue...

2000	$24.15	52.3%	$0.57	21.2%
2001	$23.40	(–3.1%)	$0.69	21.1%

Notice how after a big run (stock price up over 50% in 2000) the stock takes a breather and actually declines a little in 2001. Many investors pile into stocks or mutual funds *after* they've had a great run. It would have been better to invest when the shares were going down—as shown in 1999. However, notice how the dividends keep on rising...

2002	$27.21	16.3%	$0.76	10.1%
2003	$31.74	16.6%	$0.86	13.2%
2004	$31.70	(–0.1%)	$1.01	17.4%
2005	$41.67	31.5%	$1.18	16.8%
2006	$49.80	19.5%	$1.44	22.0%
2007	$56.04	12.5%	$1.82	26.4%

RBC is a fairly stable company with over a century of history, but the stock price does fluctuate as shown above. Earlier in 2008, RBC shares reached a low of $42.82 or an almost 24% drop from the 2007 closing price—but I simply ignored this stock price decline and focused on the dividend which has been increased again to $2.00 per share. If you had simply bought the stock at the close of 1997, you would have paid $18.84 per share. You'd now be collecting $2.00 in dividends *every year* (or almost 11% of your original investment). The stock price fluctuation has been largely irrelevant. Stock market crashes don't matter if you simply keep collecting the dividends.

You are retired so young—you might have half a century or more of not working. How will you avoid running out of money?

This is the beauty of receiving dividends and *never* selling any of your holdings. Over time, the prices of the products or services the companies you own shares in go up with inflation, and this increases profits over time. For example, have you ever seen the old advertising signs which say, "Drink Coca-Cola" and at the bottom you see "5 cents". This was the price of a Coke before I was born. Today, that same Coke from a vending machine costs $1.50 to $2.00 (equal to 30 to 40 times as much).

In addition, many established companies are continually reinvesting a portion of their earnings back into their businesses, which tends to accelerate profit growth even more. Sticking with the Coke example, at the time Cokes sold for only 5 cents, you could only buy it in the US and a handful of other western countries. Over 80% of humanity had not yet tasted their first Coke. Contrast that to today where Coke is served in over 200 countries around the world. So it's all pretty simple. Wouldn't a company that sells Cokes for $1— $2 in over 200 countries around the world earn more money that a company that sells Cokes for only 5 cents and only in a handful of countries? That's why I buy and then simply hold on and collect the dividends as the company grows. It's interesting to note that one share of Coca-Cola that sold for around $40 when the company first went public is now worth millions of dollars.

Over time as the income rises, dividends also rise which means you never run out of money. In fact the reverse is true—you have *MORE* money to spend over time *as long as you never sell your stocks!*

I don't agree with the typical investment model where you sell some assets and withdraw a certain amount of your portfolio every year. Under this situation, you are drawing down your wealth—a scary proposition in my opinion. If you are cashing out a portion of your portfolio every year, even if you are retiring at a more traditional age, you might run the risk of running out of money as people are living longer than ever before. An interesting statistic is that there are more 85 year-olds alive today than have reached that age in the entire history of mankind. We're living longer—so it's wise to make sure we don't run out of money. That's why simply collecting the dividends and *never* selling your stocks is a good approach.

Isn't it risky relying on just dividend income? What if a company reduces its dividend?

Dividend cuts do happen from time to time and

if you are relying on dividends for income, you might be in trouble if the companies you own cut or eliminate their dividends. However, there are some ways to reduce this risk.

First, invest in solid companies selling recession-proof products with a long history of raising dividends following the list of criteria I outlined in *STOP WORKING: Here's How You Can!* The nine criteria are:

1 • only invest in companies you understand

2 • only invest in companies that pay a dividend (preferably a rising one)

3 • look for company stocks that are cheap

4 • invest in companies that are recession-proof

5 • invest in companies dominant in their industries

6 • invest in companies that have a long history of strong performance

7 • invest in companies that have customer loyalty

8 • once you've bought the perfect company—never sell!

Remember, 95% of stocks are not worth owning at any price, so only buy the best quality and hold on—and watch the dividends increase over time. This can be really powerful! For example, suppose you bought shares in Johnson and Johnson 20 years ago—one of the companies I've highlighted in the past. Look at how the dividends have grown over time:

Year	Dividends per Share
1988	$0.12
1989	$0.14
1990	$0.17
1991	$0.19
.... (years pass).......	
2003	$0.93
2004	$1.10
2005	$1.28
2006	$1.46
2007	$1.62

The dividends have grown by over *13 times (from 12 cents to $1.62)* or at a rate of almost 14% per year! I shortened this chart for simplicity, but it is interesting to note that JNJ has increased dividends for 46 consecutive years—a good track record. Most of my holdings follow similar patterns. That's what I look for—companies with solid historical dividend growth. By owning several companies in different industries, even if one or two cut their dividends, the other companies keep raising the payout—and raising the amount of money flowing to you.

Second, don't most people rely on a paycheque from only *one* employer? Remember, even in good times companies restructure and lay off workers—so you never know exactly how stable your paycheque is. If dividends are getting cut the company is usually in deep trouble, thus your job is even less secure. So how would relying on an income from *just one company* (your employer) be safer than relying on income from *many different companies*—the companies in your portfolio? Does your paycheque rise at almost 14% per year (as the dividends above have risen)?

How do you know what to invest in?

Most of the best investment ideas are companies whose products or services we use regularly. However, we often miss what is directly in front of our nose. I'd like to use an old story to illustrate this idea:

Many years ago there was a maintenance guy who worked at a major department store. Every day he wheeled a wheel barrow out the front door with all his work tools inside. The security guard just "knew" the maintenance guy was a thief. So every day the security guard would stop him and go over everything with a fine tooth comb making sure he wasn't ripping off the store. Every night the maintenance guy would carry his work tools back into the store, smile at the security guard, and say goodnight. This went on for years until finally one day the maintenance guy was retiring.

On the very last day, the security guard begged the maintenance worker to tell him how he been stealing—explaining that everything was in the past and there would be absolutely no repercussions.

The maintenance guy smiled, then answered, "There was nothing stolen hiding in the wheel barrow which you checked every day. I was stealing wheel barrows."

The point is that we often overlook what is directly in front of our face—and there are good opportunities all around us. A recent personal example is Rogers Communication—which is the largest voice and data communications company in Canada, the largest cable operator, and also a huge media owner (and the owner of the Rogers Centre—formerly the Sky Dome in Toronto). During the 1990s, Rogers kept buying various assets, assumed massive amounts of debt and was hardly a generous dividend payer—so my mind switched to "ignore" any time I saw any information about Rogers. But in recent years the company has been paying down debt and hiking its dividend generously.

Think about it—this is essentially a "one-decision" company. You subscribe *once*, then you simply pay your bill by sending the company money every month for the rest of your life. If you want to have internet, phone, cable, cell-phones, etc in Canada there are only a few choices—and Rogers is one of them.

From a business perspective, it cost billions of dollars to create the networks to offer services such as cable or cell phones and money is lost for a long time. This is because the number of subscribers is not high enough to cover the incredible costs of building a massive network. The beauty is that once you reach the magic number of customers to break even, each incremental customer costs you very little—its huge profit! The network has already been built so adding new customers is inexpensive. This is much different than selling goods that have to be produced and shipped and each extra sale results in only a small profit increase.

I never thought about this aspect until I was discussing investing with a friend of mine and he mentioned that he uses Rogers and mentioned he pays them a large amount every month and how it must be a good investment. Upon research, I had to agree. I had to "unlearn" my bias against Rogers that I had from earlier times when it was a debt-ridden, stingy dividend payer and reevaluate my position. So keep looking right in front of your nose for good opportunities—or simply track everywhere you spend money for a month or two and invest where you spend that money. Remember to stick with companies whose products or services you would still use even if your income was cut in half—the "recession-proof" test and only look for those companies a grade 1 kid could understand. Simplicity and profitability often go hand in hand.

How has your portfolio done since retirement? What have been your best and worst investments?

I covered how my portfolio dividends have done since retirement in *The Lazy Investor*, and I've done that again in the chapter that follows this one. Simply, there have been additional dividend increases with no dividend decreases since my last update and I have not sold any of my holdings.

As far as the best and worst investments—why

don't we look at the worst one first? By far the worst performing stock I bought before retiring was Weston. It has declined from around $100 a share when I bought it to the current price of around $50 (a 50% drop). This company has a huge bakery business across North America and is also the controlling shareholder of Loblaws (the largest grocery retailer in Canada). This is a perfect example of hindsight being 20/20 as this stock has been clobbered by two factors that would have been hard to predict at the time I made the purchase.

The first blow to this company came a few years ago with the sudden rise in the popularity of the Atkins diet (a low-carb eating plan). This was a huge hit to the bakery division of this company. As people moved away from eating high carbohydrate foods, they bought less bakery products.

The second and much larger hit to Weston was the announcement by Wal-Mart that it was going to offer groceries across Canada. In the US market Wal-Mart has decimated the grocery retailing industry and stolen so many customers that it is now the largest grocery retailer in the US. Loblaws (majority owned by Weston) had to take action or else Wal-Mart would steal their customers too. So as a preemptive measure, the company started selling non-grocery related items such as clothing

and kitchenware. It also tried to restructure to reduce costs. The company's plan seemed to be to
compete with Wal-Mart by offering a wider selec-
tion of products and reducing their prices. However there were many problems with the execution
of the strategy and company profits declined.

Finally they seem to be changing their strategy.
From the commercials and advertising I've seen, it
seems the strategy now is to reposition the company as a greener, more quality-oriented company
with the tag-line "Worth switching supermarkets
for". I have no clue whether this change in direc-
tion will pay off, but I do know that the company
owns a number of locations where it operates its
stores and it is still the owner of two highly re-
spected brands in Canada (President's Choice and
Loblaws). Of course it would have been better to
have not bought the stock a few years ago, but selling now would be like closing the barn door *after*
the horse has already left!

So how has this worst performer affected my
retirement income? Well regardless of the fact that
the stock price has plummeted 50%, the dividend
has remained constant. That is the beauty of the
dividend-based retirement strategy.

I remember reading Peter Lynch (a great investor I followed in the creation of my investing ideas) where he mentioned something to the effect that if you buy 10 stocks—two will underperform your expectations, two will outperform, and the rest will perform in line. The basic idea is that everyone makes mistakes from time to time but the overall effect of wealth accumulation still encourages owning stocks.

This leads me to my best investment. In my first book, *STOP WORKING: Here's How You Can!* I discussed the importance of oil to modern society and addressed a theory called "Peak Oil". I also offered a few potential investment candidates. My best investment was Canadian Oil Sands.

I originally bought Canadian Oil Sands for $40 a share and it paid a $2 dividend, which worked out to ($2 divided by $40 = 5%) at that time. Since then the stock price has risen to over 5 times the original price I purchased it at. These massive share price gains dwarf the losses suffered from my worst investment (Weston). However, as I focus on dividends rather than share price, these gains are not important to me. The real story is the income I receive—the dividends being paid. The original $2 dividend has grown relentlessly—to the current $20 a unit every year!

Think about it—for a one-time payment of $40 to buy a share, *I will now earn $20 every single year—forever!* I will simply continue to hold this investment and collect the dividend cheques as they arrive.

Don't you get bored? What do you do all day?

This is one of the surprising questions I get asked. Part of my thinking is that time is so much more valuable than money and I want to spend my time as best I can to make myself happy. I understand that some people love their work—but let's be honest—a lot of people don't. A quick look at a survey done by *The Globe and* Mail in 2007 indicated that 15% of people found their jobs "extremely boring" while 30% felt stuck in "dead-end jobs" and 38% said they work "just to make money". In reality, if working was always a lot of fun, they wouldn't have to pay people to do it! I agree with Ronald Reagan when he said, "They say hard work never hurt anybody, but I figure why take the chance."

Even if you really love your work, by having the financial means—you can *choose to work or not!* Choices are a good thing. By not being financially forced to work, you free up your time to do things you really enjoy. There are so many things in life I'd like to do, how about you? Why spend your precious time doing things you don't enjoy simply to pay the bills?

Why don't you believe in RRSPs? Don't you understand the benefits?

This is the most controversial aspects of my retirement strategy as I left the workforce without even owning an RRSP and followed that up with a chapter in my first book entitled, *"RRSPs? No Thank You"* The point I was trying to make was that RRSPs are over hyped and one should make sure that this is the best route for them—sometimes it isn't. The financial industry has many incentives to get you to invest in an RRSP but I feel you should question whether or not they are *your* best option. Here are the key statements I made about RRSPs:

1. It may be better not to contribute if your income is below $32,000.
2. Although contributing to an RRSP can be a great move, so is paying off your mortgage early.
3. Borrowing money from a paid off home and investing it can be a better strategy than buying RRSPs.

4. RRSPs can be used to split income between spouses to lower the overall taxes a family has to pay.

Investing in an RRSP depends on your personal circumstances and much could be written on that topic alone, but it is outside the strategy I am trying to outline in this book. You have to look at your own situation, but for me, RRSPs were not the route I took.

Isn't not owning any fixed income investments (such as bonds or GICs) risky?

Conventional investment wisdom argues that a certain portion of your portfolio should be invested in fixed income such as bonds or bank GICs. My personal portfolio is 100% equities (company shares) as I am in my 30s and my biggest concern is my income not being able to grow fast enough over the long-term to keep up to or beat inflation. Many people say that everyone should own some bonds because they are less risky than stocks—but in my opinion they are in fact *more* risky. Let me explain why using a simple example. Suppose you invest $1,000 in a 30-year govern-

ment bond and it pays 5% per year. Under this scenario you would pay $1,000 up front for your bond
and collect ($1,000 x 5% = $50) per year in interest.
You would collect this $50 every year for 30 years
guaranteed and at the end of 30 years you would
get your original $1,000 back—also *guaranteed*.
Stocks don't offer that certainty, so how could
bonds possibly be more risky than stocks? Simple—prices rise over time due to inflation.

Let's use a simple product to illustrate this. Suppose right now donuts cost $1 each. When you in-
vest $1,000 dollars in the bond from above, you are
essentially taking an amount of money that would
normally buy 1,000 donuts. For this investment, you
are earning $50 per year in interest (or 50 donuts
worth of interest as donuts are currently $1 each).

However, inflation happens over time and prices
tend to rise. From our example, if donut prices rise
3% per year (a reasonable long-term average rate
based on history), even though you are still earning $50 every year, the number of donuts you can
buy decreases over time because they are more expensive every year. Here's a chart to show you how
focusing on fixed income and buying bonds will
not lead to wealth creation using the donut example and assuming prices rising 3% per year:

Year	Interest Collected	Cost per Donut (rise 3% per year)	Number of Donuts You Can Buy
1	$50	1.03	($50/1.03) = 48.55
2	$50	1.06	($50/1.06) = 47.17
3	$50	1.09	45.76
4	$50	1.13	44.42
5	$50	1.16	43.13

** Many years pass with donut prices rising at 3% average **

Year	Interest Collected	Cost per Donut (rise 3% per year)	Number of Donuts You Can Buy
26	$50	2.16	23.18
27	$50	2.22	22.51
28	$50	2.29	21.85
29	$50	2.36	21.22
30	$50	2.43	20.60

When you first bought your bond, $50 bought 50 donuts as donuts cost only $1 each. When you receive your first interest payment after one year, you have only earned enough to buy 48.55 donuts as they now cost $1.03 each due to inflation. By the time you have had your money invested for 30 years, you can only buy 20.60 donuts with your $50 interest payment as doughnut prices have risen over the years from only $1.00 each to $2.43

each. In addition, at the end of the 30th year you also get your original $1,000 back. However this can now only buy you ($1,000 divided by 2.43 each =) 412 donuts! This might be great for your diet—but it certainly doesn't fatten your wallet!

If instead you had purchased shares in a donut company like Tim Hortons for example, the initial dividend might have been lower but the company would be making more money every year as donut prices increased. As Tim Hortons charged their customers more money and earned more profits, it would then also be in the position to raise its dividend every year which would keep up with donut prices! Bond interest is fixed and that's why I consider bonds to be too risky for me.

If you really want to keep some fixed income in your portfolio, buy inflation-protected bonds. However, over time you will create more wealth by owning quality stocks. The next chapter will look at which stocks I've most recently invested in.

Updating my personal Portfolio Moves

"I never worry about action, but only about inaction."
Sir Winston Churchill

It's been over four years since I retired at 34—and a few things have changed in my portfolio. In *The Lazy Investor* I outlined the changes I had made to my portfolio since retirement up to that point, so here I will simply mention what changes I have made since then. So here are the stock purchases and sales I've made since my last update:

Deletions from Portfolio

None. My goal is to buy and never sell, and I have simply been collecting my dividends and have not found a reason to sell any of my positions.

Additions to Portfolio

- Bank of America
- Starbucks
- Wal-Mart (added more shares to my position)
- Lowes

At the time of this writing, there have been four new additions to my portfolio. Besides these additions, I have sold many put options on a variety of stocks I'm hoping to buy which I will cover in the next chapter. You might notice that the above investments are all US companies. When I wrote *"STOP WORKING: Here's How You Can!"* I argued for keeping the bulk of one's assets in Canada. I mentioned (page 59):

> *"Canadian governments have gotten their collective financial houses in order while the US has not, so you might even see a gradual rise in the value of the Canadian dollar. In fact, the Canadian dollar was worth more than the US dollar as recently as the 1970s.*

There is an old expression that says if you give an infinite number of monkeys an infinite number of typewriters, eventually all the great works of Shakespeare will be produced. Similarly if enough economists make enough predictions, some of them will turn out to be correct. When I mentioned that the Canadian dollar might rise against the US dollar over four years ago—it was simply mentioned as a possibility—and it turned out to be true. However, I don't feel I have any predictive powers and I could have just as easily been wrong in my prediction.

Although I like to keep the bulk of my assets right here in Canada, I like to have some exposure to large US companies for greater diversification. When I first retired, I had very little exposure to US companies because our dollar had been so low that it was too expensive to buy them. With the Canuck Buck rising to reach parity, I've taken the opportunity to add some US positions—and will continue to do so if I can find some more gems. Here's my thinking on these purchases:

Bank of America

Banks make money—it's that simple. Bank of America is the largest bank in the US and is in the position to benefit from the credit crisis as weaker banks will fold or be bought out—and banks like Bank of America will gain market share. As one of only 58 dividend aristocrats (companies with 25 or more consecutive annual dividend increases), this bank has a habit of paying dividends. It will be hurt in the short-term because of the economic situation south of the border, but longer term it will do very well.

Starbucks

There are few companies with globally recognizable brands that have no peer competitors and are on track for total world domination within their industry—but Starbucks is one of them.

Starbucks is the largest purveyor of coffee in the US with over 8,000 locations. Seattle's Best Coffee is the number 2 coffee retailer, which opened its 500th store in June of 2007. Starbucks is a Goliath compared to Seattle's Best Coffee. More surprisingly, Starbucks owns Seattle's Best Coffee. Try to think of another company with this type of domination of an industry—a definite rarity.

There are currently 500 stores in China with an eventual goal of 5,000.

I've spent time in Korea and one of the things I've noticed is that consumers there want to have the "best" and don't mind paying a premium to get it. I've often used my experiences in Korea as a "litmus test" to see which products might work in China—as the two countries have many cultural similarities.

Eventually this company will mature, growth will slow and by that time the free cash flow generated will be many times larger than it is today.

At that time, dividends should be paid adding to my income stream. Since my current dividend holdings have hiked their dividends so effectively, I'm willing to wait while this new dividend machine is assembled.

Wal-Mart

This company has more sales every year than most countries' entire GDP. It's the lowest cost provider and largest grocery retailer in the US. As times get tough, people shift to cheaper alternatives and Wal-Mart fits that bill.

Wal-Mart became a public company in 1970—the year I was born. If anyone had invested $10,000 in the company then , it would be worth over $100 million today. Heck, even $100 would have become a cool million dollars. The company is not going to grow as fast in the future, but it's still a pretty solid company which has increased dividends every year since it went public.

Wal-Mart's main goal is to be the cheapest retailer for many items. I go there often to shop—especially for kids stuff. The store is always crowded with the cash registers ringing away. One of only 58 companies in the US with 25 or more years of consecutive dividend increases, I was happy to add more shares of this stock at cheap prices.

Lowes

A lot of Canadians are not familiar with Lowes, but it is the "other" massive home improvement retailer in the US and is similar in many respects to Home Depot. With the problems with the housing market in the US, both Home Depot and Lowes have had a rough time the last few quarters and their stock prices have been beaten down. Regardless, the US population is still growing quickly. In fact, the total US population recently surpassed 300 million and it is projected to reach 400 million by 2043—in only 35 years. I'm going to guess that longer term, all these people are going to need places to live and this will be good news for Lowes and Home Depot. The interesting thing is that Lowes appeals to women. Even though men do most of the actual home repairs in North America, it is women who have the most impact in making the decisions. So Lowes is well-positioned in this regard and it has been gaining market share over the last number of years.

Earnings have been growing at over 20% per year for the last 10 years and this company should profit handily once the housing market recovers. Although it retains most of its profits to fund additional growth, it's relatively small dividend has been growing over time. I'm happy to have had the opportunity to add this holding to my portfolio at good prices.

And now the important part of the story....

How is the dividend income doing with my strategy? Below is a list of the holdings I've owned since I retired and how the dividends have done:

Algonquin Power Income Fund	** no change **
Canadian Oil Sands Trust	UP 900%
Corby Distilleries	UP 10% (see note below)
Enbridge Income Fund	UP 11%
Encana Corp	UP 300%
Johnson and Johnson	UP 61%
Livingston International	UP 28%
Manulife Financial	UP 85%
Pembina Pipelines	UP 37%
Pengrowth Energy	UP 4% (see note below)
Riocan REIT	UP 11%
TransCanada Power	** no change **
George Weston	** no change **

** Notes:

Corby paid an additional special dividend of $1.50 (equivalent to $6.00 per share pre-split) in early 2007

Pengrowth paid a very high initial dividend, but it probably won't grow over time...regardless, I am earning approximately 18% per year dividend income off my initial investment

Overall, my income from these holdings has increased substantially faster than inflation as 10 of the 13 original holdings have increased their dividends. So far, the strategy is working extremely well.

In my last book, I also listed the 4 stock holdings I had added since retirement. They included:

Consumer's Waterheater
Pfizer
Royal Bank of Canada
Wal-Mart

Each and every one of these new additions to my portfolio have increased dividends since I purchased them. With all the dividend increases, my disposable income keeps rising and the strategy is working well.

MAKING MONEY FOR NOTHING—REAL LIFE EXAMPLES

"Formal education will make you a living; self-education will make you a fortune."
Jim Rohn

The stock markets—especially US stock markets have been in a state of turmoil for a few years at the time of this writing. This offers up opportunities for investors to profit. As the old saying goes, "You make money when you buy".

The weakness in the US markets coupled with the very strong Canadian dollar has given me an opening to offer to buy some stocks at very cheap prices. Using the put-selling strategy discussed earlier, here are some of the options I sold and a list of some of the stocks I'm hoping to pick up cheaply. Notice a lot of them are for stocks I already own shares in—sometimes the best shares to buy are in companies you already own shares in.

- Bank of America
- Starbucks
- Johnson and Johnson
- Wells Fargo
- Kraft
- Sysco
- US Bancorp
- Lowes

Let's take a quick look at a few of these:

Following the money

I sold puts at $30 and $35 for Bank of America. With the premiums I collected, my actual price will work out to $30.10 or $26.80 if I get to buy them—almost 50% off their high price. With a current dividend of $2.56, I'd collect dividends between 8.5% and 9.5%—with a great record of growth as mentioned above. The same general logic follows with Wells Fargo and US Bancorp—very stable and profitable banks. I sold puts in US Bancorp at $20 and $25, and also sold puts in Wells Fargo at $20. It also doesn't hurt that Warren Buffett has been buying shares in these banks as well.

Turning Caffeine into Cash!

Over many centuries a number of alchemists spent their entire lives trying to find the secret to turning lead into gold—without success. However, Starbucks has found the formula for turning caffeine into money with amazing success. With thousands of locations all over the world and people lining up to pay $4 for a cup of coffee, the profits keep growing! Profits are 80 times what they were in the early 90s—and there's more growth to come. The stock price reached a peak of $40 per share last year, then fell hard. I sold puts for prices of $17.50 and $15, and pocketed $1.65 and $2.65 for my efforts. If I buy the shares, I'll be getting them for around $14.85 or $13.35 each—over 60% off the high price!

Making people "Healthy and Wealthy"

I've covered Johnson and Johnson's illustrious past in my previous books, so I won't rehash too much here. However, this company is the most diversified health care company in the world selling products with growing demand because of aging populations. I hope these shares go down and I can buy them, but unfortunately it seems I'll just be pocketing a little free money here—around $4.00 per share if the price stays above $60. Oh well, I already own shares.

Krafty Moneymaker

Kraft is one of the world's largest food companies with a range of brands that people use every day. Warren Buffett has bought a lot of shares and owns a pretty sizeable stake in the company. I sold put options at $25 which would be a very cheap price. If I don't get to buy the shares (which seems very likely), at least I make a little free money. I pocketed $2.20 for each option I sold, so my actual price would work out to under $23 per share if I buy them.

Everybody Has to Eat

People have to eat (usually three times a day) and as more people dine out, Sysco makes more money. They provide all the basic products for many restaurants, hotels, hospitals. Who do you think provides the essentials like the little packets of sugar, ketchup, etc? Sysco has turned this seemingly boring business into stellar profits. I sold options and earned a premium of $2.05 a share. I still hope it drops to my strike price of $25 per share so I can own some shares. This company is also one of the highly-regarded "dividend aristocrats" with over 25 consecutive years of dividend increases.

No Place like Home

I bought shares of Lowes (similar to Home Depot but growing faster) in the low 20s and I also sold put options at $15 each. I don't know how pessimistic people will become with the imploding housing market in the US, but if there is an extreme overreaction, I would be happy to get some of these shares for a super cheap price. I earned $1.50 per share for these options, but I'm hoping to buy the shares.

"Putting it all Together"

If all my options were expiring today, the only company I would be forced to buy at current market prices would be Starbucks at $17.50. Please remember that this is at current writing and this reality will probably change by the time you read this book. If this is how things unfolded, I would use some of the premium money I received to buy these shares and I would still have thousands of dollars left over which I would have earned for free. In other words, I would pocket "Money for Nothing" and still get my Starbucks "stocks for FREE!"

I'm hoping between now and the time my options expire that a few more stocks move down in price so that I can buy them at cheap prices. The best thing that could happen is a major stock market correction where I can buy all the stocks I sold put options on—as I would be adding to my portfolio at very good prices. Then I could start collecting the generous dividends—which would increase my income. If this doesn't happen and I can't buy any of the shares I wanted, I'd simply keep the thousands of dollars I've earned in option premiums for free! Either way it's win-win!

Someone you know could benefit from reading

Money for Nothing

It makes the perfect gift for any occasion.

Order online at:

www.stopworking.ca

Order toll-free at:

1-888-686-7867

$19.95 • FREE Shipping!
We accept Visa, MasterCard and American Express!

Special Offer!

Complete Financial Literacy Set:

1. *The Lazy Investor*
2. *STOP WORKING: Here's How You Can!*
3. *Money for Nothing*

Those with financial literacy have a huge advantage over others. This set offers the complete information anyone needs to financially succeed!

$49.95 (complete set of 3 books) • **FREE Shipping!**

Quantity Discounts:

Quantity	Price/Copy
1	$19.95
2–4	$17.95
5–9	$15.95
10–19	$13.95
20–50	$11.95
Over 50	$ 9.95

All Quantity Discount prices **include FREE shipping!*

RECOMMENDED SOURCES OF ADDITIONAL INFORMATION

"I am learning all the time.
The tombstone will be my diploma."
Eartha Kitt

STOP WORKING: Here's How You Can!
Derek Foster

The Lazy Investor
Derek Foster

The Wealthy Barber
David Chilton

One Up on Wall Street
Peter Lynch

Beating the Street
Peter Lynch

Stocks for the Long Run
Jeremy Siegel

The Future for Investors
Jeremy Siegel

The Warren Buffett Way
Robert Hagstrom

The Intelligent Investor
Ben Graham

Common Stocks and Uncommon Profits
Philip Fisher

The Money Masters
John Train

Hot Commodities
Jim Rogers

www.berkshirehathaway.com (Warren Buffett's Letters to Shareholders)
Warren Buffett

Canadian Moneysaver Magazine
(various information from many writers)

* These books are simply some suggested readings. Some of the information may be out of date. You should always seek professional advice related to tax, investment, financial, and legal issues before taking any action on your own.